D1270321

WITHDRAWN

ATCHLEY, Robert C. The sociology of retirement. Schenkman (dist.
by Halsted, a div. of Wiley), 1976. 158p il tab bibl 75-19248.
12.50. ISBN 0-470-03597-8. C.I.P.
Provides needed visibility for retirement as a transitional life stage. Unfortunately, this is an area that has not been treated adequately to date.
This book explores the historical evolution of and the preludes to retirement, along with some of its social and financial consequences. Although billed as a sociological treatment of retirement, it is more
broadly based and includes suggested areas of research and training,
future retirement patterns, and a brief theory of adjustment to retirement. It is a comprehensible, succinct, and well-written book, unlike
some of the readers in retirement, such as Frances M. Carp's *Retirement*
(1972). A major strength is its approach to retirement as a process, not
a dichotomy. There are some proofreading errors in misplaced commas
and misspelled words. Excellent bibliography; chapter notes and sum-
maries; large print; few figures. Recommended for undergraduate and
graduate libraries.

NOT P

THE
SOCIOLOGY
OF
RETIREMENT

With growing numbers of people facing retirement, this book serves a vital need. Too little comprehensive material on the subject is currently available. The author of this distinguished volume hopes that **The Sociology of Retirement** will "help people retire better than they otherwise might have, work their way into retirement preparation programs, and spark some new directions from retirement research."

Dr. Atchley not only defines retirement from a historical perspective; he brings it into sharp focus as it affects the individual socially, biologically, psychologically, and financially. With a spiralling unemployment pattern it follows that more and more people will be affected by retirement which, according to the author, may be viewed as "a process, as an event, as a social role or as a phase of life." However viewed, it is an aspect of social man, and therefore the more we know about it, the better. It is just as important to know about the retirement stage as it is to know about adolescence or old age, and hence the importance of Atchley's work.

THE
SOCIOLOGY
OF
RETIREMENT

by
ROBERT C. ATCHLEY

107252

Schenkman Publishing Company Inc.

HALSTED PRESS DIVISION
JOHN WILEY AND SONS
New York — London — Sydney — Toronto

Copyright © 1976
Schenkman Publishing Company, Inc.
Cambridge, Massachusetts 02138

Distributed solely by Halsted Press, a Division of
John Wiley & Sons, Inc., New York.

Library of Congress Cataloging in Publication Data

Atchley, Robert C
  The sociology of retirement.

  Bibliography: p.
  1. Retirement. I. Title
HQ1062.A8   301.43'5   75-19248
ISBN 0-470-03597-8

TABLE OF CONTENTS

- redistribution of population
- reduction of unemployment
- *differential consequences*
  - sex
  - social class

- general reactions to retirement
- factors in successful adjustment
- is retirement a crisis?
✓- a theory of retirement adjustment

- economic support for a growing retired population
- impact of aging older population
- manpower fluctuations and retirement policy
- retirement and the individual
- research needs
- training needs
- program needs

PREFACE

This book is designed to do three things: to provide a conceptual framework through which retirement can be viewed as a complex and evolving social phenomenon, to summarize the research literature on retirement, and to identify conspicuous gaps in our knowledge about retirement. In my opinion, to understand retirement one must view it from several vantage points. Accordingly, this book examines retirement from a number of "slants."

Writing this book has been fun. I hope that some of the "thrill of discovery" I felt as I worked my way through some of the unchartered territory will rub off onto the reader. I hope also that the reader will gain from the book a balanced view of retirement as a phenomenon that can have positive outcomes. Finally, I hope that some of the ideas presented in this book will help people retire better than they otherwise might have, work their way into retirement preparation programs, and spark some new directions in retirement research.

I have been helped along the line by many people. Helena Lopata deserves credit (or blame) for prodding me into doing the book in the first place. Gordon Streib and Erdman Palmore gave me some very useful comments on the first two chapters. I benefitted a great deal from being able to try out drafts of the book on classes at the University of Southern California's Summer Institute for Study in Gerontology in 1973 and again in 1974. These classes were just the right mixture of graduate students, practitioners, and retired people to give the book a useful acid test.

FIGURE 1. Relationships Among Age, Life Cycle, Occupational Cycle, and Family Cycle.*

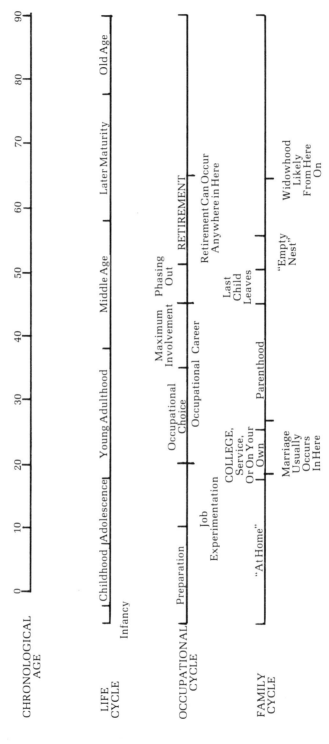

*These relationships fluctuate widely for specific individuals.

1 • Introduction

Retirement has steadily grown in importance in industrial societies. In seventy-five years, retirement in the United States changed from a rare and novel social pattern to a practically universal social institution. Retirement can be viewed in several ways—as a process, as an event, as a social role, or as a phase of life. It can be viewed as both a cause and an effect. It is a complex social pattern that touches the lives of almost everyone. Consequently, knowing about retirement is just as important to a comprehensive knowledge of social man as knowing about adolescence, middle age, occupational career or any other phase of the life cycle.[1]

This book concerns the *sociology* of retirement. It deals with those aspects of retirement that people have in common by virtue of the fact that they live out their lives among other people in a material and symbolic culture. It also deals with the role retirement plays in the operation of a complex society. The book is mainly about retirement in the United States. Information about retirement in other countries will be brought in at various points, but for the most part the American experience will be the central focus.

Retirement is a condition in which an individual is forced or allowed to be and is employed less than full-time (whatever that may mean in his particular job) and in which his income is derived at least in part from a retirement pension earned through prior years of service as a job holder. Both of these conditions must be met for an individual to be retired. For example, many career military personnel leave the service only to begin another full-time job. Thus, while these people draw pensions and receive other retirement benefits, they are not retired in the least. Likewise, many workers lose their jobs in later years and cannot find another. Yet until they reach the minimum age, they cannot draw retirement pensions and must therefore be classed as unemployed rather than retired.

Retirement thus refers primarily to the final phase of the occupational life cycle. It refers to the period, following a career of employment, in which occupational responsibilities and often opportunities are at a minimum and in which economic wherewithal comes at least in part by virtue of past occupational efforts. The employment necessary to make retirement possible need not be continuous. For example, many women work during young adulthood, withdraw while their children are small, and return to work later on. In the United States, persons born after 1951 need work only ten years on a job covered by Social Security in order to qualify for a retirement pension at age sixty-two. Of course, the amount of service and level of earnings influence the amount of the pension. Various aspects of retirement income are dealt with in detail in a later chapter.

The most essential characteristic of retirement as a social institution is that the norms of the society allow an individual, by virtue of the work he performs on the job, to establish a right to an income without holding a job. And this income in turn gives the individual the opportunity to play the role of retired person.

In discussing retirement, I will take great pains to consistently relate retirement to the concept of the *job* rather than to the concept of *work*. No one could seriously contend that retirement means an end to work, because work is a very general term which encompasses the exertion of energy toward a wide variety of particular ends. A person's job, on the other hand, refers more specifically to his position of employment. The job connotes work performed for pay, and it is this linkage of position and pay that is crucial to understanding retirement.

Because retirement requires a certain amount of prior employment, it roughly corresponds to the later stages of the life cycle—middle age or later maturity (Tibbitts, 1960). As we shall see later, adequately playing the retirement role requires adequate physical and financial resources to allow the individual to maintain his independence. And since old age is characterized symptomatically by extreme frailty and disability and increased financial and physical dependency, most people cannot play the role of retired person very long after they begin to exhibit the symptoms of old age. Note that here we are not talking about chronological age, but symptomatic age [Atchley and George, 1973]. An individual can be in his nineties and still play the retirement role, so long as he remains free of the symptoms of frailty and disability that characterize old age. Figure 1 very roughly illustrates how retirement relates to chronological age, the life, cycle, other stages of the occupational cycle, and the family cycle.

Technically, retirement can begin anytime the individual has amassed enough pension credits or capital to provide a living without holding a job. For most people, however, retirement before age fifty-five is not economically feasible. Accordingly, retirement generally begins during the latter part of middle age or later. Most people's children are grown and off on their own by the time retirement begins. Also, most people retire several years before mortality begins to make widowhood widespread. We shall often need to bear in mind that the "empty nest." widowhood, and physical decline are only sometimes part of the social situation in which the individual experiences retirement.

Apart from being a phase of the occupational cycle, however, retirement can also refer to an event, a process, or a social role.

Looking at retirement as an event means focusing on the point of public separation from the job, usually via some sort of retirement ceremony. However, in many cases there is no ceremony or definite point of separation. Many people "retire" from one occupation only to take up another. Sometimes the individual leaves or is laid off from one job and finds that as a result of age discrimination he cannot get another. People may also retire in stages by keeping a part-time job.

Retirement is not a dichotomy: retired vs. not retired. It is a process that begins when the individual realizes that some day he will leave his job and ends when he becomes so feeble or impoverished that he can no longer play the retirement role. Retirement is a process through which the retirement role is approached, taken up, learned, mastered, and relinquished. Looking at the retirement process also means looking at the maze of possible ways in which retirement may fit into an individual's life.

Looking at retirement as a social role means focusing on the rights, duties, and relationships associated with the position of "retired person." Being a retired person is a definite position in American society, and there is widespread agreement concerning what kind of behavior to expect from retired people. There is less agreement as to what retired people can expect from others. We shall have a great deal to say later about retirement as a social role since this is a central element in several theories of retirement as well as much of the retirement research.

By now it should be obvious that retirement is indeed a complex subject, and before we finish we will have dealt at some length with each of the aspects of retirement mentioned in this section.

The Sociology of Retirement

Sociology is an accumulation of ideas, including some we call "facts," about what exists in the social world and why. Looking at the form, content, and results of human life in groups, the sociologist tries to make explicit—to describe and explain—the structure of the social world, how and why it changes, and how we influence and are influenced by it. As C. Wright Mills (1959) put it, "The sociological imagination enables its possessor to understand the larger historical scene in terms of its meaning for the inner life and the external career of a variety of individuals . . . (It) enables us to grasp history and biography and the relations between the two in society." (Ibid., pp. 5-6)

Sociology is also an academic discipline in which ideas about the social world are organized into a very loose structure which makes them easier to test, accumulate, or transmit. Sociology is made up of language and knowledge. Language provides symbols for communication and is also the basis for the classification systems used to diagnose and label the patterns sociologists observe. Because it rests on language, sociology is always culture-bound, tied to the world-view of those who decide what is and what is not "real."[2] Knowledge consists of systematic description and explanation. Sociological knowledge is usually called scientific only if it has been empirically verified.

But what is sociology for? Who uses it and for what purposes? Everyone who lives in the social world can benefit from knowing more about it. Mills put it this way:

What ordinary men are directly aware of and what they try to do are bounded by the private orbits in which they live; their visions and their powers are limited to the close-up scenes of job, family, neighborhood; in other social [settings], they move vicariously and remain spectators. And the more aware they become, however vaguely, of ambitions and of threats which transcend their immediate locales, the more trapped they seem to feel . . . .What they need, and what they feel they need, is a quality of mind that will help them to use information and to develop reason in order to achieve lucid summations of what is going on in the world and of what may be happening within themselves. (1959, pp. 3-5).

The promise of sociology is thus to help society understand itself and to help the individual understand how his life influences and is influenced by the society he lives in.

Accordingly, a sociology of retirement must place retirement in the historical development of industrial society. It must also show how retirement fits into the lives of individuals and how the individual and society interact concerning retirement.

Here are some of the basic questions which a sociology of retirement must answer:

—What is retirement? What differentiates it from other social patterns? For example, how is retirement different from unemployment?
—What are the conditions necessary for the development of retirement as a societal pattern? What historical forces combine to produce it? For example, why did retirement not appear before the 19th century?
—What are the consequences of retirement for society?
—What are the consequences of retirement for individuals?
—How does retirement relate to other social patterns and why? For example, how does retirement affect marriages?
—What factors determine the nature of the transition from work to retirement and why? For example, what role does employer policy play in the timing of retirement decisions?
—What conflicts arise between the individual and society over retirement and how are these conflicts resolved. For

example, what happens if the individual wants to retire and society doesn't want him to; or if the individual wants to keep his job and society wants him to retire?
—What are the norms which govern retirement? For example, what is expected of a retired person? When is it seemly to retire? Under what conditions can an employer justify compulsory retirement?

These and similar questions form the basis for the sociology of retirement presented in the remainder of this book. Trying to map an area of social life is a more personal thing than one might suppose, particularly in areas such as retirement where no one approach has become customary. Choosing what is important and what is not is never as objective a process as one would like.

Some Problems in Studying Retirement

Retirement presents the would-be researcher with some unique problems that sociologists in general do not have. Retirement is a relatively recent phenomenon, and, as with most newborns, change is rapid in the first stages of development. Students of retirement are thus quite concerned with whether the information and inferences from ten-year-old research are still useable. Also, the recency of retirement means that comparative, cross-national studies of retirement are not very widespread. It also means that the number of research gaps is much larger than that for areas such as the sociology of formal organizations which have been widely researched for decades. Nearly all research on retirement has been done since 1950.

There are also some troublesome problems when it comes to operationally defining retirement. Operational definitions seek to define an abstract conception such as retirement in terms of simple, observable procedures. "Retired person" has been variously defined:

—as any person who performs no gainful employment during a given year.
—as any person who is receiving a retirement pension benefit.
—as any person not employed full-time, year round.

Palmore (1967) found that, among men sixty-five and over,

64 percent had no work experience in the previous year, 80 percent received some kind of retirement benefit, and 87 percent worked less than year-round, full time. Thus, the way retired person is operationally defined makes quite a difference in who can be included and in the number of people defined as retired.

Classifications of retirement have ranged all the way from oversimplified dichotomies (retired vs. not retired) to very complex systems. Palmore (1971) has used what is probably the most sophisticated classification system to date. Using weeks *not* worked as the criterion for "degree" of retirement, Palmore was able to establish various "retirement rates."[4] He found, for example, that among people sixty-two or over the average retirement rate for men was 35 weeks not worked and for women was 47 weeks. Palmore's findings are discussed in more detail in Chapter 2.

Another problem in studying retirement is finding a sample. Scientists almost never study the entire universe of phenomena. Instead they seek a *representative sample* of that universe. Probability samples are used by social scientists to insure that their descriptions and explanations are based on representative samples. The problem is, however, that in order to draw a probability sample, the investigator must have a *sampling frame,* a concrete representation of the universe he[5] wants to sample. Sampling frames can be either a list of names which approximates the universe or a list of addresses from whence the universe can be sampled, since presumably almost everyone lives somewhere. However, the address gambit can only be used if the characteristics which define the universe are widespread. You wouldn't take a random sample of households in San Francisco if you were looking for retired people. Too much wasted effort.

It is possible to add questions on retirement to larger studies which do use probability sampling. This technique offers the greatest prospects for gaining representative information on retired people. However, since the retirement aspect could be no more than a small part of a larger study, the questions on retirement would have to be few in number, and this factor would greatly limit the amount of detailed information on retirement that could be gathered by this means.

On the other hand, representative lists of retired people are almost impossible to come by. One of the best in the United

States is the list of Social Security pensioners, but even it doesn't include many people who are receiving other types of government pensions, railroad pensions, or those who worked in occupations not covered by Social Security. Not only that, but the Social Security beneficiaries list can *only* be used for research conducted by the Social Security Administration. Fortunately, the Social Security Administration has an ongoing program of research on retirement which provides a great deal of information (Bixby and Irelan, 1969). But, unfortunately, this research has thus far been very limited in scope, dealing mainly with economic issues.

There are few other lists which can begin to approximate the universe of retired people, however defined. As a result of sampling difficulties, retirement researchers usually settle for the sample they can get rather than the sample they would like to have. And the sample they can get usually comes from union rolls or from lists of people employed by or receiving pensions from a particular company. Accordingly, retirement research has sorely neglected people in small business, in marginal occupations, and in elite occupations. It has also neglected the poor and members of minority groups. These gaps have not occured because social gerontologists[6] are stupid or lacking in insight or methodological sophistication. The major problems have been the difficulty of the task and the scarcity of resources for research.

Despite these methodological difficulties, there has been a flurry of retirement research during the past decade or so. Two large-scale sociological studies are particularly important. Streib and Schneider (1972) studied 1,969 workers who eventually retired from a wide variety of jobs. Their study was longitudinal, and as a result, can tell us a great deal about changes that occur in individuals upon retirement. Cottrell and Atchley (1969) studied 3,533 retired people in blue-collar, white-collar and professional occupations. This study used a wide variety of measures which are useful in assessing the prevalence of various characteristics among the retired. This book will rely heavily on these studies plus a few others (Tuckman and Lorge, 1953; Friedmann and Havighurst, 1954; Simpson and McKinney, 1966; Barfield and Morgan, 1969; Havighurst, et al., 1969; and Palmore, 1971, 1965) which form the backbone of our empirical knowledge concerning the social aspects of retirement. Hence, it is finally possible to begin to construct a sociology of retirement based on empirical research rather than arm-chair deduction. However, the methodological problems mentioned earlier mean that one must be especially cautious that accepting the research results uncritically. In addition, as we shall see, there are sizeable and serious gaps in our research information on retirement.

Thus retirement is many things. As a phase of the occupational cycle, retirement is a period, following a socially defined minimum period of employment, in which occupational responsibilities and often opportunites are at a minimum and in which the individual is entitled to an income by virtue of his past occupational efforts. As an event, it is the point at which withdrawal from full-time employment is publicly announced. As a process, it is the transition from a full-time, year-round job to the role of retired person. And as a social role, retirement is the rights, duties, and associations of people who occupy the position, retired person.

Normally retirement corresponds roughly with the later maturity phase of the life cycle and with the post-childbearing phase of the family cycle. However, individuals vary widely on the degree to which the timing of events on the job, in the body, and in the family coincide. Therefore, general statements about the relationships between retirement and other aspects of life have very low predictive validity for the lives of specific individuals.

The sociology of retirement deals with the evolution of retirement as a social pattern, with the conditions which led to the development of retirement, with the consequences of retirement both for the society and for its individuals, and with the dynamics of retirement.

Despite some serious problems in defining retirement, of finding adequate ways to sample retired people, and despite the large number of research gaps, there has been enough study of retirement in recent years for us to begin to outline a sociology of retirement.

2 • Background and Evolution of Retirement

Retirement is a creation of industrial society. In the pre-industrial era, people did indeed stop working as a result of old age, but there was no way that a person could earn the right to an income without doing a job or owning enough property to provide it. It is not possible here to detail all of the complex conflicting processes through which industrialization laid the foundation for the emergence of retirement. However, it is possible to discuss some of the outcomes of industrialization which helped set the stage.

In very early societies, older people were supported only so long as they could perform some sort of productive function. People in these societies lived a difficult life, and there was seldom a surplus of food, clothing or shelter. They simply could not afford to support "dead weight." "For example, if the Eskimo grandmother could no longer even chew [hide for] the boots of the family, she would be abandoned or walled up in an igloo to await death" (Donahue, Orbach, and Pollak, 1960).

The advent of agricultural society brought two important developments: an economic surplus and the concept of property. When an ecomomic system produces more than is necessary to keep the producers of basic goods and services alive, then an economic surplus exists which can be used to support more than basic production. In agricultural societies the size of the surplus is large enough that mechanisms must be found to settle disputes over it. *Property* is a set of rules which define the rights of individuals or groups to control the use of some object, resource, or activity. Thus, in agricultural societies land became property, and control over the economic surplus

10

the land produced depended on property rights. How property rights developed is a complex issue which cannot be dealt with here. Suffice it to say simply that in agricultural societies, older people who had gained property rights could usually support themselves in old age.

For example, in the early days of American society, homestead land was given or sold very cheaply to people on the assumption that they would develop it and put it into agricultural production. When a homesteader began to grow old and experienced difficulty in doing heavy work, he usually had sons or sons-in-law to whom this responsibility could be delegated. Thus, property rights made it possible for the older homesteader to decrease gradually the amount of energy he put into the farm without losing control of what the farm produced. Because he controlled the division of labor on the farm, it was seldom necessary for the older farmer to quit producing entirely. Also because he held the power of ownership, it was technically impossible for anyone to force him out. For the rare person who lived to grow old in agricultural America, it was possible to have one's cake and eat it too. That is, if one owned property, then one could keep the demands of work at a minimum and still claim the rewards of ownership.

Those who lived to become old tended to be from the upper economic strata in which economic power had traditionally been used to support people who did not hold jobs—a leisure class. But what of the working man who failed to gain property rights? To begin with, these people did the heaviest labor and were least likely to live to be old. If they did grow old, however, they had to continue full-time work as long as they could. And when this was no longer possible, they had to fall back on the benevolence of family and of the more well-to-do members of the community. Fortunately, the ethic of conspicuous consumption meant that being able to afford to support destitute members of one's family or of the community brought status to the wealthy. Nevertheless, many older people were cast out by their families and ended up in alms houses, or they simply died of malnutrition or neglect.

Industrialization brought many changes. In the first place, industrial forms of production drastically increased the available economic surplus. The productivity of industrial America is so great that there are genuine problems of being able to consume enough of what is produced to prevent widespread unemployment. The main reason for this increase in productivity was man's discovery of ways to transform the vast pools of nonhuman energy (mainly fossil fuels) into forms that could be used to produce goods and services.[1] Today, human beings contribute far less than 1 percent of the energy used in industrial societies. This increase in available energy meant that industrial societies could support more people at a higher standard of living and still have a surplus left over for additional industrial development.

Not only did industrialization allow economies to produce more things, but it also allowed them to produce better things. Some crucial examples are food storage facilities, transportation networks, and sanitation systems. The scientific and rationalistic thought that formed the backbone of industrial technology also resulted in more knowledge about *human* machinery. As a result of increased knowledge concerning nutrition and sanitation, industrial societies were able to cut death rates significantly. This not only produced rapid population growth but also, by lowering infant mortality drastically, allowed a much larger proportion of the population to survive into old age. As urbanization increased and fertility rates declined, older people also became an increasing proportion of the population.

Cowgill and Holmes (1972) surveyed several less modernized nations, and found that in all societies, older people are transferred to activities that are less strenuous and physically exacting—to roles that are more advisory or supervisory. However, they also found that in the societies they surveyed, older people tended to retain power through control over land and the use of land. Older people also retained power as a result of religious beliefs which place elders in the strongest position to influence the supernatural.

Industrialization upset this sort of system. For one thing, with a larger proportion of older people, there simply were not enough honorific positions to go around. When only the fittest survived to become old, the old were indeed an elite who had shared economic and political advantage and who knew a great deal about the workings of the society. In industrial societies, however, people from all walks of life survive in large numbers to become old, and the old are no longer mainly from the elite. In addition, industrialization reduced the power of older people by divorcing management from ownership and by putting a lower premium on experience. And as it modified our ideas about the supernatural, the scientific revolution destroyed the role of elders as bridges to dead generations.

Industrialization also brought with it new forms of social organization. The detailed division of labor in industrial production created tremendous demand for coordination and rationalization of labor and it also created the concept of workers as reasonably standardized and interchangeable cogs in an overall system. The small-scale farmer and small businessman were replaced by the salaried worker as the backbone of the middle class.

The corporate bureaucracy became the dominant organizational form in the economy, and the growing power of the private sector produced the government bureaucracy as a means of protecting the public interest. Unions developed because labor's interest and the public interest, as pursued by government, did not necessarily coincide. As coordination *within* the economy became a strong national need, the national state came of age in industrial society as a mediator between the corporations and the unions.

The changes in social organization that accompanied the maturing of industrial society had significant impact on the lives of individuals. As the scale of economic activity increased, the power of the average individual over the conditions of his own labor declined. The rationalization and coordination of industrial labor meant that job holders had to produce up to minimum standards, and this removed the possibility of adjusting the demands of the job to fit the capabilities of the individual. The rise of the corporation and large-scale organization for production eliminated the family with its patriarchal head as the typical unit of production. The enterprising entrepreneur gave way to the manipulating manager. This paved the way for the argument that people should be relieved of their duties in old age because they were no longer capable of meeting minimum standards. (This argument rests by-and-large on myth rather than reality.) Also, the decline in owning and operating one's own business or farm meant that the vast majority of people had no way to claim an income *except* through a job. Land or other resources were no longer there for the taking, and ownership and control of the economic surplus was concentrated in the hands of large business concerns and financial institutions. The growth of stock companies meant that ownership was so divided that ownership became divorced from control over production. During this period, the working person was relatively powerless to protect himself or his family from the vagaries of the business cycle.

However, in the early part of the twentieth century, social reform movements created two strong organizational forms to oppose the monopoly of control that business concerns exercised over the economic surplus: the strong national government and the industrial union. National government generally affects the distribution of the economic surplus through laws and taxation. In this respect, the right of the national government to regulate commerce by law and to tax individual and corporate incomes and to tax the withdrawal of natural resources, especially energy resources, were important factors which tended to divorce control over the economic surplus from the ownership of resources or the means of production. Unions gained a share of control over the economic surplus because the detailed division of labor characteristic of industrial societies handed workers the power of the strike. As long as the necessary jobs can be filled by anyone and there are large numbers of people clamoring to fill them, as is often the case in agricultural societies, then strikes are not possible. But once labor becomes very specialized and requires a modicum of skill, then the collective threat to withdraw labor brings genuine power.

Industrialization also helped divorce the concept of work from the concept of life itself. *Craftsmanship* was the ideal of work in the preindustrial era. The craftsman pursued work as an end in itself because he was master of both the product and the process of creating it. He could thus learn from his work and use it to develop his own skills and capacities. The craftsman's way of livelihood influenced his entire life-style; there was no separation of work and play or work and culture (Mills, 1956: 220). Of course, even in preindustrial societies, not everyone by any means enjoyed the degree of integration of work and life-style that typified the craftsman.

However, there is nothing inherent in work that makes men love it. If it is satisfying, man loves work; if it is unsatisfying, he does not. A job may be thought of as delightful, as a bounden duty, or as a necessary evil. And the nature of the job itself plays an important part in the way man regards it. Industrialization reduced the job for many people to a fragment of a process. For workers in corporate or government bureaucracies, jobs moved toward being an element of life which was partitioned off from family and community life and which was pursued mainly as a means of gaining income instead of being a craft around which one's life revolved. The terms, job and occupation, developed out of the need for more neutral terms which did not imply the idea of a calling as the words, vocation and craft, tended to do.

A corollary trend which also helped to divorce the concept of work from the concept of life itself was the growth of the secular city. In the heyday of Calvinistic Protestantism, it was supposedly sinful to do anything that was not work. Even sexual intercourse was unethical unless it was work directed toward producing a child. Clearly, this conception of work was taken with a grain of salt by many if not most people even then, but the rise of secularism and the pluralism of values it encouraged meant that work began to lose its preeminent position in the society's *professed* value system.[2]

For all of these reasons, the stage was set for the development of retirement in the maturing industrial society. People were living long enough to contribute their necessary work in the economy and still have several years left over. In fact, since 1900 the average number of working years increased just as fast as the average number of years in retirement. The economy was productive enough to support a sizeable number of adults without jobs. In capitalist societies there was incentive to restrict the size of the labor force. The decline in the birth rate meant a smaller proportion of children drawing on the economic suplus. The rise of the national state and the labor union had made it possible for part of the economic surplus to be diverted to support people not in the labor force. This made pension systems possible. The rationalization of labor, the decline of entrepreneurship, and the rise of the secular city meant that it was not always possible nor necessarily desirable for the individual to hold a job into old age. And this made it possible for people to begin to accept without guilt the concept of retirement as an *earned right*.

This fairly abstract model of how retirement developed is based roughly on the experience in the United States, but its essential elements apply to any industrial society. Thus, the following are *necessary* conditions for the emergence of retirement as a social institution:

—People must live long enough to accumulate a socially defined minimum number of years service on one or more jobs.
—The economy must produce enough surplus to support adults who do not hold jobs.
—There must be some mechanism (such as pensions or social security) to divert part of the economic surplus to support retired people.
—People in the society must be able to accept the idea that one can legitimately live in dignity as an adult without having a job.

The easiest way to demonstrate the development of retirement empirically is to look at labor force participation rates through time for older people in the population. Table 1 is a time series for the United States which shows the labor force participation rates for men of "retirement age" or more in relation to the rates for the age group just prior to "retirement age," and several indicators of degree of economic development from 1890 to 1970. This table clearly illustrates that the decline in labor force participation of older men has been closely associated with a rapidly rising Gross National Product, a growing concentration of population in urban areas, and a dramatic increase in the use of non-human energy for production. At the same time, there has been only a slight drop in labor force participation among men in the ages just prior to sixty-five. Clearly, industrialization and the incidence of retirement have been closely related in the United States, and this same pattern has prevailed in other developed countries. Labor force participation rates for older men in less developed countries are generally more than double the rates in more developed countries.

Table 2 shows labor force participation rates for older men in several industrial societies during the period 1920-1960. This table illustrates two important points. First, each of these nations has experienced a decline in labor force participation rates for older men. Second, there is wide variation in the extent to which older people still participated in the labor force

Table 1. Percent of Males in the Labor Force for Selected Age Groups, Percent of the Total Population that is Urban, Per Capita Gross National Product, and Electrical Power Used by Commerce and Industry: United States, 1890-1970.

	Percent age 65 or over in labor force	Percent age 55-64 in labor force	Percent age 45-64 in labor force 1	Percent of population Urban	Per capita Gross National Product	Electrical power used by commerce and industry*
1970	25.8	81.5	—	73.5	4754	885.0
1960	32.2	85.2	—	69.9	2788	460.0
1950	40.4	—	88.2	64.0 a)	1876	189.0
1940	42.2	—	89.4	56.5	761	85.0
1930	54.0	—	91.0	56.2	740	75.0
1920	55.6	—	90.7	51.2	835	37.7
1900	63.1	—	90.3	—	231	15.0
1890	68.3	—	92.0	—	210	—

*In billions of kilowatt-hours

a) 4.4% of the increase from 1940 to 1950 was due to a change in the definition of urban.

Sources: U. S. Bureau of the Census, *Historical Statistics of the United States*, Washington, D. C.: U. S. Government Printing Office, 1960, pp. 71, 139, and 511; U. S. Bureau of the Census, *Statistical Abstract of the United States*, 1971, Washington, D. C.: U. S. Government Printing Office, 1971, pp. 17, 211, 308, and 501.

Table 2. Percent of Males Sixty-five or Over in the Labor Force for Selected Industrial Nations for Selected Dates: 1920-1960

	1920	1925	1930	1935	1940	1945	1950	1955	1960
Germany		47.4		29.7 a)		36.7 b)	26.8	22.9 c)	
Belgium			45.3			24.7 d)			9.8 c)
France	66.8 e)		59.2 f)			54.6 b)		40.5 g)	30.2 h)
Great Britain			47.9				3.4		
Japan			63.0		61.9				54.5
United States	55.6		54.0		42.2		4.4		32.2

a) 1933   f) 1931
b) 1946   g) 1954
c) 1961   h) 1962
d) 1947
e) 1921

Sources: P. Bairoch, et. al. *La Population Active et sa Structure*, Brussels: l'Institute de Sociologie de l'Universite Libre de Bruxelles, 1968; S. L. Wolfbein and E. W. Burgess, "Employment and Retirement" in *Aging in Western Societies*, E. W. Burgess (ed.) Chicago: University of Chicago Press, 1960, p. 66; U. S. Bureau of the Census, *Statistical Abstract of the United States: 1968*, Washington, D. C.: U. S. Government Printing Office, 1968, p. 216; and U. S. Bureau of the Census, *Historical Statistics of the United States*, Washington, D. C.: U. S. Government Printing Office, 1960, p. 71.

as of 1960. For example, the decline in the labor force participation for older Japanese is only a fraction of the decline among
older Belgians.

There are several factors which influence the extent to which
people take advantage of retirement, even in societies which
allow it. The adequacy of pensions and the extent to which
employment policies restrict employment opportunities for
older workers through mandatory retirement policies are two
key factors. Another is the existence of discrimination against
older workers which can reduce labor force participation of
older people, especially in times of economic slump or glutted
labor markets. Finally, personal factors such as health or
preference for leisure over job holding, or inability to accept
the idea of retirement also influence the extent of retirement.
The fact that Japan has a much higher labor force participation
among its older men as compared to other industrial nations
is due primarily to the inadequacy of Japanese pension systems
coupled with greater opportunities for continued employment
in farming and small business (Palmore, 1975). The Japanese
have only very recently enacted a national social sercurity
system. Reitrement tends to take place at an early age (fifty-
five or sixty) but benefits from employers are usually lump sum
payments. Social security payments in Japan are very low by
Japanese standards. As a result, most potential "retirees" are
forced to remain in the labor force. Thus, Japan has not yet
met the need for some sort of pension or insurance system to
provide incomes to retired adults, and this no doubt accounts
for much of Japan's high labor force participation among older
adults.

Retirement is certainly an established institution in the United
States. In 1967, 73 percent of American households headed by
a person age sixty-five or over reported no earnings at all during
the year, and 90 percent were drawing retirement pensions
(Bixby, 1970). Yet the extent of retirement is more than the
percent employed in the labor force. Palmore (1971) has done
probably the most definitive work to date on the problem of
measuring the extent of retirement. Using the number of weeks
not employed as a measure of the extent of retirement, Palmore
found that *total* withdrawal from the labor force was by no
means universal in any age group, yet the number of weeks
employed seldom averaged more than 18 weeks for any sub-
group of American Social Security retirement pensioners age
sixty-five or over. Table 3 summarizes some of Palmore's

findings. From this table it is obvious that the extent of retirement is influenced by age, health, and income. Palmore concluded that among the various factors which affect the extent of retirement (among those who are at all retired), age was the most important, followed by health among men and marital status among women (never-married women retired less). Obviously, retirement is often a matter of degree. Among those who have met the minimum age and service requirements necessary to entitle them to draw a retirement pension and who have withdrawn from full-time employment, there are many who not withdrawn from employment completely. A great deal more

Table 3. Mean Weeks Not Worked by Persons Receiving Social Security Retirement Benefits, by Various Characteristics and Sex, United States: 1963

Characteristics	Total	Males	Females
Total age 62 or over	42	35	47
Age:			
62-64	29	17	40
65-69	41	34	46
70-74	46	41	49
75-79	47	44	50
80-84	50	48	51
85 or more	51	51	51
Self-rated Health:			
Good	38	28	46
Fair	42	39	47
Poor	49	48	51
Income:			
$ 0- 999	48	45	50
1,000-1,999	35	41	48
2,000-2,999	34	42	49
3,000-3,999	31	35	46
4,000-5,999	37	28	45
6,000-9,000	35	26	45
10,000+	34	19	47

Source: Palmore (1971: 273 adapted).

research is needed to identify the various patterns of partial retirement and the factors which influence partial retirement. Palmore's research is an interesting, but preliminary, step in that direction.

Summary

This chapter has established that retirement is a corollary of industrialization. But unless people live long enough to accumulate the necessary service and the society has an economic surplus which can be used to support them, and some mechanism exists which can collect part of this surplus for use in providing pensions, and people can accept the idea of life without a job, retirement will not develop even in industrial societies. And even if retirement is possible, whether large numbers of people can take advantage of it depends on the adequacy of pension benefits, employment policies, the general level of health in the older population, and the value people place on having a job.

In addition, it is useful to consider retirement as a continuous variable and to think in terms of the extent of retirement. Data for the United States have shown that 69 percent of those who draw Social Security retirement benefits are totally retired and that the extent of retirement is related mainly to age, health (for men), marital status (for women), and income. However, much more research is needed in this area.

3 • Preludes to Retirement

Retirement is a relationship between people and jobs. The earned right to a continued income comes by virtue of employment, not some abstract notion of work or of social contribution. Millions of housewives spend a lifetime working but never earn the right to an income without working simply because being a housewife is not a "job" for which one receives "pay." Thus, to understand the processes which precede retirement it is necessary to examine how people relate to their jobs, how they come to expect retirement, how they feel about leaving their jobs, and how they prepare for retirement.

People and Jobs

Many professionals in industrial societies hold a highly romanticized view of the meaning of holding a job. To them, the meaning of their vocation is the meaning of life, and work is embued with the spirit of craftsmanship referred to in the previous chapter. This romanticism has often led sociologists to assume that the job is the central focus in the lives of those who have jobs, and that retirement must necessarily result in a loss of meaning in the individual's life. Many early retirement studies were so bent on studying this "pathological" aspect of retirement that other possibilities were often ignored, particularly the positive outcomes of retirement. Yet Friedmann and Havighurst (1954) quite rightly pointed out that jobs can serve many functions and have many meanings for the people who hold them. Table 4 represents some of the possibilities. Obviously, for most people the job serves a combination of these functions, and the emphasis on certain functions may

22

change over a job career. For example, early in a professional career the job is a source of status and gives direction to one's life. But usually the job brings high income, recognition, autonomy, or self expression only after a lengthy apprenticeship. Thus, from the day he begins his first job, the functions and meanings of employment for an individual are more or less in a process of evolving. This evolution continues even long after retirement. For this reason, the individual's job history is an essential underpinning which sets the stage for retirement.

Table 4.
The Relation Between the
Functions
and Meanings of Work

Work Function	Work Meaning
1. Income	a) A way to achieve minimum subsistence.
	b) A way to achieve a higher level of living.
2. Expenditure of Time and Energy	a) Something to do.
	b) A way to fill time.
3. Identification and Status	a) A source of self respect
	b) A way to get recognition from others.
	c) A way to define one's role in life.
4. Association	a) A determinant of friendship.
	b) Relationships with co-workers.
	c) Super-subordinate relationships.
5. Source of Meaningful Life Experiences	a) Gives purpose to life
	b) An outlet for creativity and self expression.
	c) A source of new experience.
	d) A way to be of service to others.

As Streib and Schneider (1971) point out, it is a gross over-simplification to call industrial societies "work oriented." Jobs range from hod carrier to supreme court justice; some involve working with congenial colleagues, others involve reading meters on transformers; some jobs do not pay enough to live on, others pay enough for many people to live on; some jobs provide for an orderly career progression, others require frequent changes of job in order to "advance." Under these circumstances it is highly doubtful that there is enough equivalent meaning among jobs to allow one to speak of the meaning of the job in general. However, by examining various occupational *categories*, it is possible to arrive at some general statement concerning the meaning of jobs within large occupational groups. For example, Simpson, Back, and McKinney (1966c) divided jobs into upper-white-collar jobs, middle-stratum jobs (lower-white-collar and upper-blue-collar), and semiskilled jobs. Upper-white collar jobs such as those held by executives, professionals and government officials provide the greatest rewards. Not only is the pay usually high, but so are recognition and autonomy. These jobs also usually involve highly skilled tasks and/or a great deal of responsibility. These jobs also tend to demand involvement in the affairs of the larger community in addition to simply performing the jobs.

Middle-stratum jobs such as clerk, salesman, skilled worker or foreman are quite varied in terms of rewards. Some are satisfying; some are not. In general, these jobs tend to lack the pattern of systematic advancement which typifies upper-white-collar jobs. There is often high job turnover, low work autonomy, little recognition, and no demands that necessarily involve them in a sphere of interests off the job. Semi-skilled jobs such as factory worker or service worker tend to offer few rewards other than sociability and subsistence, especially if the job is in a bureaucratic organization.

Friedmann and Havighurst (1954) found that among blue-collar workers (steel workers and coal miners) money was by far the most often mentioned meaning of work. Very few blue-collar workers saw their jobs as sources of meaningful life experiences. Retail sales workers saw their jobs as providing a routine, associations, and purposeful activities. Physicians saw their jobs in terms of service to others and only secondarily in terms of associations.

The type of job has a strong impact on the degree to which the person becomes committed to it and on the orientation the job holder takes. Simpson, Back, and McKinney (1966c:80) found that the upper-white-collar jobs tended to foster a high degree of commitment toward the job, while middle-stratum and semi-skilled jobs tended to attract a low degree of commitment from job holders. Upper-white-collar job holders also tended to be oriented toward intrinsic aspects of the job such as autonomy, self expression, or new experience while middle-stratum and semiskilled job holders tended to be oriented toward extrinsic aspects such as pay, job security, or friends on the job.

Obviously, the relationship between a person and his job is a complex question which cannot be easily summarized by terms such as "work oriented." Industrial societies present such a variety of quite different jobs with varying degrees of ability to attract people to them that it becomes ludicrous to label an industrial society "work oriented." In fact, most of the jobs in industrial societies fall into the middle-stratum and semiskilled categories in which a high degree of commitment toward work is not typical. However, since most of the people who study and write about such societies are holders of upper-white-collar jobs, it is understandable, if not forgivable, that they should see the entire society as being like them—highly committed to jobs that are intrinsically satisfying.

The language used to describe conditions of employment reveals a great deal about the orientation expected of a person in a given situation. For example, *profession* refers to positions which generally require a great deal of preparation and which involve mental rather than manual dexterity. Having a profession also means that people expect a certain amount of long-term dedication to one's position of employment. *Craft* refers to positions of employment which demand the exercise of exceptional skill. Implicit in the idea of a craft is also a certain amount of dedication and long-term commitment, since, crafts generally require lengthy apprenticeships. *Job*, on the other hand, is a word which refers to any sort of gainful employment, be it regular or temporary, full-time or part-time. There is no implication in the idea of a job that the job holder will be committed to or dedicated to his position of employment. In industrial societies, the overwhelming majority of people have *jobs* rather than *crafts* or *professions*.

The work of Williams and Wirths (1965) sheds some important light on the question of the pervasiveness of highly job-oriented life style. Working with the sample from the Kansas City Study of Adult Life, Williams and Wirths classified their subjects into six life styles according to judges' ratings of the subjects' areas and degrees of major self investment and involvement. These life styles were called: world of work, familism, living alone, couplehood, easing through life with minimal involvement, and living fully. Williams and Wirths found that the world of work was the central element in the life style for only 15 percent of their subjects.

Using data from the Scripps Foundation study of retired teachers and telephone company employees, I examined the prevalence *in retirement* of a positive orientation toward the job (Atchley, 1971). Work orientation was defined in terms of measures of work commitment, job satisfaction, and work as a self value. Contrary to what I expected, a high degree of positive work orientation was not present in most of the people in our sample. Every category but that of retired women teachers showed that the majority had a low degree of positive work orientation, and in no category did the percentage with a high degree of positive work orientation exceed 15 percent. From this I concluded that earlier investigators, including myself, were wrong to assume that years on the job would automatically produce an identification with and a commitment to the job which would last even after retirement.

Accordingly, the assumption that people in industrial societies are highly committed to and oriented toward their jobs—one of the key assumptions of much of the early retirement literature—is now being called into question. It is true that there are jobs in industrial societies which do involve the concept of craftsmanship mentioned earlier, and these jobs do tend to attract a strong commitment and affect the life style of the job holder even off the job. But such jobs are only at a small fraction of the job market in industrial societies. The overwhelming majority of jobs are routine and unchallenging positions which people fill mainly in order to get the money necessary to do other things.

A witness of the U. S. Senate Special Committee on Aging (1967) hearings on retirement and the individual put it well:

> I worked for the Ford Motor Company for 41 years. I took
> an early retirement at age sixty-two. I had intended to talk

just about Social Security benefits and the fact that they are frozen, but if the committee would permit me, I would like to digress just a bit to cover some of the remarks I heard here prior.

One thing that really disturbed me was a remark made here a short time ago by one of the witnesses that factory workers, do they really know whether they want to retire or not? Another remark that quite shook me up was the fact that maybe some of these people love their work. Now I could understand a person in a chosen profession, and most of the witnesses have been professional people—I could understand them having a love for their work, but I think that the gentlemen on the platform understand as I do, that working in a factory, which includes about 95 percent of the people on Social Security, is not a matter of choice. When you go into a factory, it is a matter of assignment. They say, "Do this," and you are assigned to a machine and this is what you do and you repeat it over and over and over, the same little routine operation. There is no diversification and absolutely no opportunity for knowledge or exchange or anything else-you just stand there all day long, day after day, year after year, for a lifetime. And then somebody asks you, "Do you really want to retire?"

Practically every person working in a factory today want to retire. The only deterrent to people retiring from factories is whether they are going to get a pension on which they will be able to live and support their wife or other dependents in the mode or manner in which they have accustomed. That is the only deterrent.

So when the Big Three came along with $400 a month, I immediately retired. There was no question in my mind of whether I wanted to retire or not. It was only a question of having enough to retire on, live in some semblance of dignity, and not become a burden on your family or a burden on the community. That's the big thing with a person retiring from a factory.

Much more research is necessary in order to know the exact nature of the links between people and their jobs. However, it is safe to say that in industrial societies there are many possible patterns and that, at least in the United States, the "world of work" life style is seldom the prevalent one. Certainly how the individual feels about his job has an impact on how he will view the prospect of retiring. The important point is that this impact does not take place in a vacuum but occurs instead in the context of the individual's own personal situation.

The link between people and jobs is not only one of commitment but also one of mutual influence. Kohn and Schooler (1973) found that jobs which involved the exercise of self-direction in terms of freedom from supervision, substantively complex work, and a non-routinized flow of work tended to cause people in those jobs to value self-direction and to have an orientation toward themselves and toward the outside world which emphasized self-direction. Simpson, Back, and McKinney (1966a) found that professional jobs tended to be oriented around *symbols*, middle-status jobs tended to be oriented around *people*, and semiskilled jobs tended to be oriented around *things*. They also found that skills involving people showed the greatest carry-over from the job into retirement. In short, jobs often teach people orientations or skills which can be used in a variety of settings off the job. As we shall see later, to the extent that jobs teach people self-direction, intellectual flexibility or sociability, they in effect prepare people for the demands of retirement.

The Meaning of Retirement

Osgood, Suci, and Tannenbaum (1957) pioneered the study of semantic meaning. Using their techniques I did a preliminary study of the meaning of retirement (Atchley, 1974). I found that retirement is an overwhelmingly favorable concept which consists of four separate dimensions: activity, moral evaluation, emotional evaluation and physical potency. People tended to see retirement as active, involved, expanding, full, and busy; as fair and good; as hopeful and meaningful; and as healthy, relaxed, mobile, able and independent. The activity dimension was the only one that showed even the slightest departure from completely positive, and even it showed over 70 percent of the respondents in the most favorable categories. These dimensions held regardless of age, sex, occupation, education, marital status, or willingness to continue on the job.

Ash (1966) studied how the concept of retirement was legitimized among steelworkers. He found that in 1951 retirement was justified only if the individual was physically unable to continue, but by 1960 retirement was being justified as a reward for a lifetime of work. Thus, the concept changed from something to be avoided to a sought-after reward.

Attitudes Toward Retirement

While the job itself has an impact on how people feel about leaving it, the idea of retirement is also an object of people's attitudes. Attitudes toward leaving one's job and attitudes toward retirement are not the same, although they are related.

Most people take it for granted that they will retire someday. However, very little research has been done concerning just when in the life cycle this conclusion is reached. But most adults do expect to retire sometime in their sixties, and nearly half would like to retire sooner if they could. Only a small proportion (less than 10 percent) expresses dread of retirement (Riley and Foner, 1968).

Attitude toward retirement depends largely on the financial outlook. Acceptance of retirement is no doubt tied to the fact that most people anticipate no financial difficulties in retirement, even though most expect a substantial reduction in income. Among those who expect a low income, however, only about a third are favorable toward retirement. Attitudes toward retirement tend to be most favorable among people who hold higher-level, upper-income jobs. However, there is some evidence that favorable attitudes toward retirement decrease somewhat at the upper professional and white collar levels.

Yet the nearer people are to retirement age the less likely they are to favor retirement (Riley and Foner, 1968). This seeming paradox probably stems either from the fact that those nearing retirement have a more realistic view of the often stark economic realities of retirement income, or that those nearer retirement (and therefore older) were reared in an era in which retirement was less acceptable.

Jacobson (1972) found that British workers with physically demanding jobs were twice as likely to favor retirement as compared to those with lighter jobs. He also found that freedom on the job was inversely related to willingness to retire.

There is also some evidence that as retirement becomes more accepted and as its meaning shifts to one with fewer negative implications, an even larger proportion of the work force will favor retirement. The cohorts who were retiring in 1970 were much more favorably disposed toward retirement than those who retired in 1960 or earlier. How an individual feels about retirement is certainly related to what he has been taught to feel about it and there are certainly cohort differences in what people have learned about retirement. However, there is also an element in an individual's attitude which probably stems from the way retirement fits into the context of his particular life. More research is needed on these aspects of attitudes toward retirement.

Prominent government officials, executives, and professionals usually must commit themselves to a "world of work" lifestyle. Because there are only so many hours in a day and because their careers demand most of those hours, work infuses every part of their lives. For these people, retirement has to be a profound change, and it is certainly unsurprising that such people resist retirement.

However, for most middle and upper-status job holders there is much less of this all-consuming commitment to the job. Most people at this level are reasonably well-educated and have lived lives in which their job was relegated to an isolated compartment. The remaining hours of their lives are spent developing interests and associations which are related to work only through the income it provides. That is, work is important because it provides the money which is a prerequisite for enjoying many other areas of life. This is not to say that these people dislike their jobs. Some do and some don't. It is simply that apart from the money it provides, the job is irrelevant to the person's life. Jobs in this range provide a sufficient and perhaps even excessive income, but otherwise the job brings its holder and his family no special status in the community or other rewards which might make the job a more important part of life. The attitudes of these people toward retirement are specific to the job. If they dislike their jobs, then retirement is usually quite attractive, and there is little ambivalence. If, on the other hand, they like their jobs, then they are often in the enviable position of having to choose among attractive alternatives—an attractive retirement vs. an attractive job. At this level, financial insecurities are seldom a significant influence on attitudes toward retirement.

People with semiskilled or unskilled jobs face some problems which make them tend to dislike the idea of retirement. The first of these problems is financial. While some factory workers get substantial pensions, the majority of working-class Americans face real poverty in retirement. The second problem involves alternatives to work. Assuming that everyone has to do something, the working-class individual faces retirement with a minimum of choices. His education has not prepared him to enjoy a life of leisure, and neither has his life-style. He has also tended to concentrate his leisure participation in family affairs, rather than in voluntary associations or in the community. Individuals in this category may regard the job as the lesser of two evils. They may not like their jobs, but they like them better than sitting around, doing nothing. However, the aging process affects this category harder and earlier than it does those with less physically taxing jobs, and as a result, the older the worker the more likely he is to favor retirement, even if it means a great reduction in activity. The overwhelming majority of semiskilled workers favors retirement.

In addition to occupational level, sex also has a systematic influence on attitudes toward retirement. Retirement literature is full of statements to the effect that retirement is easier for women than for men because women have the housewife role to fall back on (Cumming and Henry, 1961; Donahue, Orbach and Pollak, 1960; Williams and Wirths, 1965). Accordingly, it would be expected that women would favor retirement more than men do. However, two studies have found that just prior to retirement, women are less favorable toward retirement than men are (Streib and Schneider, 1971; Cottrell and Atchley, 1969). Streib and Schneider suggest that these unexpected findings may be due to our tendency to overestimate the male's work commitment and underestimate the female's and to the possibility that women who are still in the labor force by retirement age are inordinately job-oriented. The fact that most women can legitimately "retire" to the housewife role long before the usual retirement age, leads to speculation that for many women, "voluntary" retirement may occur much earlier than age sixty-five. It has been assumed that retirement is a problem only for men and hence little study has been made of retirement among women. Accordingly, we still do not know much about the pre-retirement attitudes of women toward their jobs or toward retirement. This is an area greatly in need of further research.

Preparation for Retirement

Preparation for retirement can be either conscious or nonconscious and either formal or informal. Conscious retirement preparation may be formal as in the case of a retirement planning course taken through a plant or office or union local, or it may be informal as in the case of the individual who simply talks to others about retirement. Nonconscious preparation can also be formal. For example, the existence of Social Security legislation guarantees a minimum retirement income, and the fact that millions of people draw Social Security retirement pensions does a great deal to heighten the individual's awareness of retirement as a social eventuality. Nonconscious, informal retirement preparation comes via such accidental means as contacts with retired persons, exposure to mass media presentations which include retired people, and exposure to folk-myths, jokes, and stereotypes concerning retirement.

Much of what leads up to an individual's retirement is haphazard and the result of his own unique biography. Yet even in the nonconscious, informal area of retirement preparation there are forces which influence people in reasonably consistent ways.

Perhaps the most prevalent consistency in retirement preparation is the lack of exposure to conscious, formal programs aimed specifically at retirement preparation. In one survey, only about 10 percent of the companies reported that they have a retirement preparation program (Schultz, 1963). This is an unfortunate fact, because retirement preparation programs generally improve the ability to plan successfully for retirement.

Exposure to formal retirement preparation programs is not a random matter. People in middle-status jobs[1] are likely to be exposed to formal programs because they tend to be favorably disposed toward retirement and, therefore, not put off by the idea of planning for it; and because they tend to work in organizations which are more apt to provide formal programs. Upper-status job-holders,[2] on the other hand, are reluctant to retire, seek to avoid information on retirement, and in fact, because they are accustomed to manipulating the environment to achieve goals, often seem to need little formal preparation for retirement.

Perhaps because of these factors, there are very few formal retirement programs aimed at upper-status job-holders apart from occasional programs on estate planning. Semiskilled workers[3] also get little exposure to formal programs, although they are generally favorable toward the idea of retirement. This is probably because most programs are voluntary and their marginal literacy and fatalistic posture toward retirement make semiskilled workers less likely to volunteer (Simpson, Back, and McKinney, 1966b).

Regardless of occupational level, a positive orientation toward retirement is strongly related to exposure to formal programs, successful retirement planning, and exposure to media presentations or personal discussions on retirement (Riley and Foner, 1968). Early retirees are also more likely to seek formal programs (Green, et al., 1969).

Exposure to formal retirement preparation programs has been shown to have several important results. First, and perhaps foremost, it reduces uncertainties about retirement. In addition, formal programs often reduce the tendency to miss one's job in retirement (Simpson, Back, and McKinney, (1966b.) Hunter (1968) found that exposure to formal programs tends to reduce dissatisfaction with retirement and worries about health, and to foster a higher level of social participation in retirement. Green and his associates (1969) found that formal programs also resulted in a more satisfactory retirement income, less belief in negative stereotypes about retirement, and better self-rated health. A surprise finding was that formal retirement programs had positive results regardless of whether the person exposed to the program thought it was useful or not. The possible effects of formal retirement preparation programs may be somewhat overstated by the research literature since there is usually a self-selection process involved in who gets exposed to such programs, but there can be little doubt that most people benefit from such exposure.

Given the results of formal programs, the relative scarcity of such programs might seem surprising. The key to the puzzle probably lies in the fact that until recently, a few employers and unions have been the only organizations sponsoring formal retirement preparation programs. Rarely do senior centers, city recreation departments, or other organizations sponsor these programs. Another problem is that many of the people who could benefit the most from formal programs do not realize it. Finally, the fact that most programs are geared for literate, middle-income people limits their usefulness to other groups. Thus, haphazard financing and administration, failure to "sell" the value of formal programs to a large segment of the employed population, and a limited target group are all factors which keep down the number of formal programs and restrict the usefulness of such programs as currently exist.

A prime issue in formulating programs is whether the emphasis should be on crisis prevention (through counseling) or on providing information and stimulating people to plan for retirement. Kasschau (1974) argues that much of the current apathy concerning retirement preparation programs can be traced back to research results showing that such programs are not very effective at performing the counseling functions. In addition, not very many people need in-depth counseling. However, the research literature supports the effectiveness of preretirement programs in providing information to participants and in encouraging them to plan for retirement. Kasschau concludes that given the limited resources and duration of most programs, the planning goal is more realistic than the counseling goal.

One of the difficulties in trying to help people prepare for retirement is the wide variety of circumstances people face. Pre-retirement counseling about finances, health, living arrangements, leisure time, and a host of other topics must be oriented to the individual's own situation if it is to be most effective. The heterogeneity of the population of older job-holders means that pre-retirement programs on a group basis can be only a first step.

It should be useful to look for a moment at the structure a retirement preparation program might take. Most of the discussion involves my own opinions, but they are generally based on research findings. To begin with, exposure to formal programs could occur in gradual increments. First, a brief orientation to the need for retirement preparation might be a part of every school child's experience. Next, at about age forty-five there might be a formal program about financial planning and creative use of leisure. Finally, just prior to retirement there might be a formal program which emphasizes legal aspects, health, housing, and work opportunities in addition to an emphasis on financial and leisure planning.

The following are some of the questions which need to be resolved by those responsible for structuring retirement planning programs:

—What is the impact of employer attitudes toward retirement on the effectiveness of retirement planning programs?
—What is the impact of how the staff views retirement on their ability to plan and direct a successful program?
—What changes have occurred recently in people's attitudes toward retirement? How will this affect retirement planning programs?
—Does everyone need retirement planning? How can those who do be identified?
—To what extent must the strategy used in retirement preparation be tailored to fit the type of person who is retiring? What criteria could be used to sort people out?
—What should the goals of retirement planning be?
—What do people see as potential retirement problems?
—Are there retirement problems that a retirement planning program cannot or should not handle?
—To what extent should retirement planning programs emphasize potential problems as opposed to presenting a balanced picture of positive and negative issues?
—How should retirement planning programs be structured?
　　—What topics should be covered? What format works best (lecture, discussion, etc.)?
　　—How old should the participants be? How close to retirement?
　　—To what extent should retired people be involved? What about other outside resources?
　　—Should there be a separate program for women?
　　—What is the optimum size for a group?
　　—How many meetings should there be? How long for each meeting?
　　—Should spouses be invited?
—How can people be encouraged to participate?
—What resources are available (experts, films, literature, etc.)?
—How do you know that the program is successful?

Obviously, the way these issues are resolved will vary considerably, depending on the needs of the particular program.

Yet even if formal retirement programs were free and available to all, and even if everyone saw their potential, there would still be a great deal of preparation for retirement that would have to take place apart from formal programs.

Simpson, Back, and McKinney (1966b) studied the extent to which people consciously seek information informally. The authors classified informal sources into four categories: retired people, fellow employees, company officials, and Social Security personnel. They found that information sources differed according to former occupational level. As expected, middle-status job-holders sought information more and from all sources, while upper-white-collar workers relied primarily on fellow workers and company officials, and semiskilled job-holders relied overwhelmingly on company officials. These patterns held up fairly well regardless of orientation toward retirement. Better than half had read something about retirement, regardless of former occupational level, but exposure to radio or television programs on retirement was much more prevalent among the middle-status and semiskilled workers than among the upper-white-collar people.

Practically nothing is known about the role of nonconscious processes in preparation for retirement. However, there can be little doubt that attitudes toward retirement and preparation for it are influenced by the symbolic content of the culture in which retirement takes place. In American society, retirement has a number of stereotypes attached to it, and many of these stereotypes are negative. True, retirement is seen by many as a time for rest and relaxation, reaping the fruits of a life's labor, and generally enjoying oneself, but it is also seen by many as leading to boredom, poverty, ill health, loss of status and friends, and premature death. Since most people favor retirement, it seems safe to assume that somehow the positive images of retirement are winning out over the negative. However, we do not know why or how this happens. There is some indication that one of the ways that formal programs enhance retirement adjustment is simply by counteracting the negative stereotypes of retirement (Greene, et al., 1969).

Gradually increasing the time spent away from the job is a particularly promising means of formal, nonconscious retirement preparation. One way this has been done is to gradually increase the length of the annual vacation after a certain age, say fifty-five. Another possibility is to gradually shorten the length of the work day. The move in many industries to four ten-hour work days per week and regular three-day weekends can also be expected to produce nonconscious preparation for retirement, since it forces the worker to deal with large blocks of leisure time on a weekly basis. It might even be desirable to have a policy of reduced pay for part of the worker's extended vacations during the five years preceding retirement to help the individual get accustomed to living on a retirement income. If begun early enough, this policy would be particularly useful because it would encourage better financial planning for retirement.

Summary

Numerous factors influence the way an individual approaches retirement. To begin with, his commitment to his job governs how he feels about leaving it. A small number of people have crafts or professions which become a way of life; others view their jobs as a pleasant but not all-consuming aspect of their lives; and still others see their jobs as a necessary evil. Characterization of industrial societies as "work-oriented" overstates the extent to which people are strongly committed to their jobs. Research results indicate that in American society, only about 15 percent of the older population has a life style which is closely tied to a job.

Most people view retirement favorably, although there is a tendency to be somewhat less positive just prior to retirement, particularly among women. Only a very small proportion dreads retirement. Financial outlook seems to be the most important single factor influencing attitudes toward retirement in America: the brighter the retirement income outlook, the more positive the attitude toward retirement. People in highly rewarding jobs tend to resist retirement. People in middle-status jobs tend to look forward to retirement, especially if they dislike their jobs. People in semiskilled jobs generally favor retirement but, because of financial fears, favor it less than people in middle-status jobs. Given a secure income, semiskilled workers are also anxious about the lack of viable choices other than the job to occupy their time.

Few people are exposed to formal retirement preparation programs, but middle-status job-holders, who tend to be self-selected from the ranks of those who already favor retirement, predominate among those exposed to such programs. Nevertheless, these programs have been found to reduce uncertainties about retirement, job deprivation, worries over health and finance, and belief in negative stereotypes of retirement. Such programs also increase social participation.

Ideally, retirement preparation would begin early, and deal with issues such as financial planning, creative use of leisure, legal aspects, health, housing, and work opportunities. Also, at least some programs would be sponsored by the public and be available to everyone, including those who work in small business or in service occupations where formal programs run by the employer are rare.

Middle-status job-holders are most likely to seek information about retirement from others, but all groups show a tendency to read articles about retirement. While we know very little about the influence of negative stereotypes on preparation for retirement, their influence does not seem to be very great, since most people favor retirement. Much more research is needed on the impact of stereotypes on preparation for retirement.

4 • The Decision to Retire

The individual usually has some leeway concerning the timing of his retirement, if indeed he retires at all. Retirement decisions take place in a concrete social situation composed of a number of elements. To begin with, the individual has specific attitudes toward retirement and toward leaving his job. These were discussed in the previous chapter. Also, the job itself often has attached to it rules concerning the minimum age at which one may retire and minimum years of service required to qualify for a pension. Rules concerning mandatory retirement age are also common. The individual's fellow workers, friends and family can also have an influence on the timing of the retirement decision. Also, the level of pension benefits is an important consideration. Finally, physical factors such as health and ability to continue to do the job also affect the retirement decision.

Rules of the Job

The individual may agree with or be at odds with the rules of his job concerning retirement. If he wants to retire and meets the rules for retirement (usually minimum age and length of service), then he will retire. But if he wants to retire, but has not met the job rules for retirement, then the inability to secure an income for his retirement will prevent him from retiring. Thus, if the individual has met the service requirement (twenty years, say) but has not yet reached the minimum age (let's say fifty-five), then he must wait until he is fifty-five to retire.

On the other hand, the individual may not want to retire. The pertinent job rule here is the mandatory retirement age. If he has not yet reached it, the individual may continue to work. However, even if he wants to continue on the job, he usually cannot if he has attained the mandatory retirement age. Employers sometimes ignore mandatory retirement rules if it is to their advantage and there is no union to oppose them, but the individual himself seldom has the power to ignore such rules.

From a societal view, rules concerning minimum length of service are justified in terms of making sure that the individual has made an adequate contribution to make it possible to support him in retirement. Mandatory retirement rules based upon age are justified in terms of the need to create opportunities for younger workers and to phase out older, presumably less-effective workers.

Of course, there are jobs, mainly in the professions and crafts, which do not have retirement rules. For example, there is no mandatory retirement age for self-employed lawyers, physicians, or proprietors. But there are jobs, particularly in the small business and service areas of the economy, which do not have pensions or retirement rules. In these cases, the rules of the public pension system operate in most industrial societies. Thus, in the United States a worker must have worked at least ten years at a job covered by the Social Security program and have reached age sixty-two in order to get a pension. Of course, there is no mandatory retirement age under Social Security.

Both the minimum service requirement and the minimum retirement age are important elements of insurance-type retirement pension systems. These systems are usually based on the balance of what is paid into the system with what must be paid out. If the individual is employed too short a time, then he will not have paid in (or have paid in for him by his employer) enough to provide a minimum pension throughout his retirement. Or if he retires too early, then he will draw on his pension fund too many years to provide an adequate pension level.

The current conventions concerning minimum service and age requirements are based on *estimates* of how much income people are willing to defer for how long in order to create retirement pension funds. In fact, most workers want to spread the cost of a pension over as many years as possible and to pay in at a level which will provide them with a pension only from about age fifty-five or sixty on. People might say they would like to retire earlier, but they probably would not be willing to reduce current income even further in order to do it.

Social Security is not an insurance-type system. The retirement pensions paid under Social Security are financed from the current contributions of those who are still paying into the system. The reserve fund is only large enough to pay one year's benefits. Under this system, the minimum age and service requirements are arbitrary and are in no way tied to the actuarial concepts which underlie the insurance-type systems. The reduced pensions which are paid to people who retire early under Social Security are also arbitrary, as is the relationship between average earnings and pension levels. Social Security is set up to *look* like insurance primarily because in 1935, when the Social Security Act went into force, the concept of insurance was easier for people to accept than was a public pension system financed through an earnings tax. In fact, most Americans probably still prefer to regard Social Security as essentially the same thing as a private annuity. All of this means that the rules for retirement under Social Security can be more flexible, since they are not tied to actuarial tables. It is important to recognize that Social Security retirement rules are based primarily on employment policy rather than on welfare policy or concepts of social insurance.

The subject of retirement income will be dealt with in more detail in a later chapter. Suffice it to say here that the service requirement and minimum retirement age, which are part of the retirement rules associated with most jobs, are conventions which are at least loosely associated with the mathematics of creating pensions.

In recent years, the phenomenon of early retirement has become more prevalent. Early retirement is usually a system under which employees are allowed to retire before they become eligible for a Social Security retirement pension. The employer or union usually provides supplemental pension payments to keep pensions at an adequate level until the retirer becomes old enough to collect a Social Security retirement pension.

For example, under the provisions of a contract negotiated in 1970 between the United Auto Workers and General Motors, employees with thirty years of service can retire at age fifty-six on a private pension of $500 per month. At age sixty-five, the private pension would drop to $171 per month as the retirer began to draw his Social Security retirement pension. His total pension income would remain at $500 per month.

Early retirement gets support from two sources. On the one

hand, there are dissatisfied industrial workers who want to retire as soon as it becomes economically feasible (Barfield and Morgan, 1969). On the other hand, employers often welcome early retirement schemes as a means of controlling the size and characteristics of their work-force. Fields (1970) found that about 10 percent of early retirements could be classed as involuntary. Employers were particularly eager to use early retirement as a means of coping with technological change, mergers, plant closings, and production cut-backs. Many employers used early retirement as a means of getting workers to do "voluntarily" what the employer wanted; i. e., leave their jobs.[1]

There is some evidence to indicate that the rampant inflation since 1973 is giving people second thoughts about early retirement. The desire to retire is still there, but the long-run purchasing power of fixed pensions is increasingly in doubt. As an example, for an individual who retired in 1967 under a fixed early retirement pension of $500 per month, by August, 1974, the purchasing power of that pension had declined to around $335! In the face of such trends, it is perhaps wise to hang on to a job if possible since wages and salaries at least have some possibility of increasing along with inflation, whereas the prospects for such increases for those drawing private retirement pensions are nil.

Mandatory retirement[2] policies seem to revolve around the problem of phasing older workers out of a complex production process in an orderly fashion. That mandatory retirement policies are the best means of accomplishing this is by no means clear.

Mandatory retirement is most often justified on the grounds that it is simple and easy to administer, that retirement "for cause" would require complicated measures, that mandatory retirement eliminates bias or discrimination in the phase-out process, and that it opens channels of promotion for younger workers. None of these arguments is especially telling. Since many if not most people retire before the mandatory retirement age, especially in recent years, an unpredictable point of retirement must also be reasonably easy to administer. If incompetence is not obvious, and, therefore, not easy to measure, then one could question how serious a problem it is. Employers consistently exercise bias in the face of mandatory retirement policies by keeping people on after the mandatory retirement age if it suits their purposes. Thus, mandatory retirement policies are not a foolproof way to eliminate discrimination. The most telling of the arguments concerns making room for younger workers. This is the argument to which older workers are most sensitive. Given that there are more people than jobs, a good case might be made for the idea that an individual is entitled to hold one only so long. However, a factual basis for this rationale has yet to be demonstrated.

Mandatory retirement has two important aspects that are less often discussed than others. One is the fact that a mandatory retirement age allows the individual a graceful exit point, a point where he can leave his job without having to admit to himself or others that he can no longer do the job. The other is that mandatory retirement gives retirement an inevitability which propels people into retirement, perhaps even before the mandatory age, who might otherwise have stayed on the job simply out of habit. However, both of these arguments have been eroded by the fact that in recent years the trend has been toward retirement as soon as possible. People no longer need an excuse to retire. It is an accepted part of life.

No one today can seriously argue that at age sixty-five or seventy, people in general are so feeble, sick, or otherwise disabled that they should be excluded in wholesale fashion from the labor force. It is questionable whether this was true even forty years ago when many mandatory retirement policies were being formulated. By definition the mandatory retirement age discriminates against an age category, and this violates the principle of equal employment opportunity. Since chronological age alone is a poor predictor of ability to perform on the job, it is an inappropriate criterion for use in implementing a mandatory retirement policy. Mandatory retirement policies waste talent and productive potential (Palmore, 1972), and in addition, are accused of forcing poverty on the retirer.

The arguments against mandatory retirement ages are, for the most part, soundly based. While the overwhelming majority of people retire because they want to and can afford it, there is a small but important minority that either does not want to retire or cannot afford to, and mandatory retirement certainly unjustly discriminates against these people. The use of age as the sole criterion cannot be defended on rational grounds. Mandatory retirement robs the individual of the opportunity to exercise his talents and skills and society is deprived of the product. Mandatory retirement ages are almost always accompanied by private pensions. Therefore, the idea that mandatory retirement forces poverty is true mainly for those not so covered or for those whose irregular work histories deprive them of adequate pensions. There are indeed thousands of older people working at jobs that have fine pension plans but who will reach the mandatory retirement age without working long enough at the same job to be entitled to a pension. Many mandatory retirement age policies are based on an erroneous assumption that retirement will not hurt the older worker financially.

On balance, there seems to be little in favor of mandatory retirement age policies. And as retirement becomes an increasingly accepted part of life, these policies will become even more unnecessary. However, there may remain cases in which mandatory retirement ages are justified, either by occupational ethics or demographic facts. Yet I see little reason to believe that mandatory retirement policies will change. There are two reasons for this. The group that is currently being hurt by mandatory retirement policies is too small to be politically effective. The majority who wants to retire may see the "right to work" faction as a threat. And the mandatory retirement age is a deeply ingrained aspect of the institution of retirement, which means that change would not be easy.

Attitudes of Fellow Workers, Friends and Family

Undoubtedly the individual's decision to retire is influenced by the informal norms of his work situation. For example, physicians are probably discouraged from retiring by the attitudes of their fellow professionals. Since retirement tends to be viewed negatively among physicians, to retire is to buck the system. On the other hand, auto workers are generally favorable toward retirement and indeed there is a growing tendency toward early retirement (Barfield and Morgan, 1969). It would be absurd to assume that two individuals anxious to retire face the same decision in these two quite different occupations.

Attitudes of friends and family also probably play an important role in the retirement decision. One man's children want him to retire, another's do not. One woman's husband wants her to retire, another's does not. One man lives in a neighborhood where retirement is sneered at, another lives in a leisure community where retirement is the rule rather than the exception. If we retire, then the characteristics that our friends and family impute to retired people will be imputed to us. All of these factors may encourage or discourage retirement, but they are almost sure to have an influence. At this point, more research is needed to establish the extent of this influence.

Other Factors in the Retirement Decision

Implicit in the concept of voluntary retirement is the notion that the individual himself has decided the time has come to retire. The rules associated with some jobs allow retirement any time between age fifty and age seventy. The rules of the job and the attitudes of fellow workers, friends and family generally either support or oppose retirement. But there are other issues which also enter into the decision to voluntarily retire.

The first of these is *income*. The prospect of a substantial reduction in income upon retirement is the primary deterrent to voluntary retirement (Riley and Foner, 1968:451). Income is the major reason people give for preferring work to retirement, yet people with high incomes usually resist retirement because of the kinds of jobs they have. Riley and Foner (1968:451) conclude that the lower prevalence of retirement among those with higher earnings may result from greater work satisfaction, better health, a higher level of material consumption during retirement, or the fact that their retirement is less likely to be mandatory.

Health is also an important factor which can influence the retirement decision, although this factor can be somewhat offset by a physically undemanding job (Steiner and Dorfman, 1957). And because jobs in industrial societies are becoming less physically demanding and the health of the older population is improving[3], health is declining in importance as a factor influencing the retirement decision. Palmore (1964:6) found that between 1951 and 1963, health declined as a reason for retirement among Social Security beneficiaries. Using a sample of auto workers who retired early with pensions of around $400 per month, Pollman (1971) asked the subjects to rank job satisfaction, fellow workers, supervision, health, retirement benefits, and desire for free time as to the importance of each in influencing their retirement decision. As might be expected, nearly half of the respondents to Pollman's questionnaire cited adequate retirement income as the primary reason for their early retirement. About 25 percent cited health as a primary reason for early retirement. Another 20 percent wanted more leisure and free time.

It is also possible that fear of leisure deters retirement. A few people have expressed concern over the fact that after elementary school, American formal education tends to neglect leisure pursuits such as art, music, and literature. Miller (1965) has theorized that implied inability to perform on the job embarrasses retired people and prevents them from engaging in leisure pursuits. However, I suspect that lack of leisure skills may be a more adequate explanation. And if an individual does lack leisure skills he can be expected to resist retirement.

The most sophisticated study to date concerning the retirement decision is Palmore's study based on the 1963 Social Security Survey of the Aged (Palmore, 1971). The sample consisted of 11,000 people who were chosen via a multistage area probability procedure which yielded a representative sample of all persons age sixty-two or over in the United States in 1963. Because of the complex sample design, each person had a differential value based on his probability of selection. In order to take these values into account in the multivariate analysis, cases were duplicated or dropped according to their weight (Palmore, 1971:270). This resulted in an effective sample of better than two and a half million people. Table 5 shows the distribution of answers given to the question: "Why did you retire?"

By using sophisticated statistical techniques, Palmore was able to analyze the relative importance of various factors in the decision to retire (assuming that more than one reason is usually operating). He found that when age, marital status, health, education, race, region, and living arrangements were examined simultaneously, age proved to be the strongest and most direct factor influencing the decision to retire for both men and women. Health was a poor second among the men, and marital status and education followed age in importance for women. Palmore concluded that there seem to be two types of reasons for retirement: *inability to work* as in the case of older age, illness, and a low degree of education; and *less need for earnings* as in the case of married women. Of these two types, inability to work appeared to be the most important reason for retirement (Palmore, 1971:282).

Yet despite the fact that Palmore's is by far the most rigorous attempt to deal with the question of why people retire, it leaves many questions still unanswered. For example, research of Pollman (1971) and by Barfield and Morgan (1969) has shown that among those who select an early retirement, adequate retirement income is far and away the most frequent reason cited. Accordingly, the fact that Palmore's study did not take retirement income into account as a factor in the decision to

Table 5. Reasons for Retirement

	Men	Women
Number (in thousands)*	1,950	772
Percentage retiring for:		
Voluntary reasons	31	58
Prefer leisure	21	20
Needed at home	1	8
Dissatisfied with job	1	2
Other	7	28
Involuntary reasons	69	62
Poor health	43	36
Compulsory retirement age	15	9
Laid off or job discontinued	8	7
Other	3	9

*Includes all persons not usually at a full-time job in 1962 who stopped their last regular full-time job since 1957. Percentages add up to more than 100 percent because some respondents gave more than one reason. Source: Palmore (1971:271) adapted.

retire is a major limitation. Also, while Palmore's work does show that age is a primary factor in the decision to retire, and that it is not merely the relationship between age and illness, education or marital status which produces this phenomenon, he is not able to specify what correlate of age does produce the effect. The fact that age is the prime criterion for mandatory retirement almost certainly has something to do with the findings. Palmore speculates that age may have two important consequences which produce decisions to retire. The first of these is prejudice and discrimination against older workers, and the second is a general societal expectation that older people *should* retire. Since Palmore's data were cross-sectional rather than longitudinal, the impact of age he observed was one of *age differences* rather than *age changes*. This means that there could well be something in the earlier socialization or historical experience of the older cohorts which would account for the age differences Palmore observed. This is a prime difficulty in trying to treat age as a causal factor without a longitudinal or cross-sequential research design.[4] There has generally been a growing percentage of voluntary retirements among those who have retired since 1962, the date of the study Palmore is reporting on. These gaps in Palmore's study would make excellent topics for further research.

We can also learn something of the decision-making process by looking at some of the literature on early retirement (Barfield and Morgan, 1969; Orbach, 1969). In a study of auto workers, Katona, Barfield and Morgan (1969:45) found that the percentage who plan an early retirement is on the increase and that planning early retirement was associated with:

—having a favorable retirement financial outlook, subjectively expressed.
—being in relatively poor, or declining health.
—having talked about "the question of when to retire" with persons outside the immediate family.
—thinking that most younger people feel that older workers should retire to provide job openings.
—preferring less work than one is now doing, or not preferring more work.
—having trouble keeping up with one's work and being unable to control the pace of the work.
—having attended at least one retirement preparation class session.

In another report of the same study, Barfield and Morgan (1969) found that of the above factors, financial ones were far and away the most important.

Orbach (1969:17) also looked at the early retirement phenomenon among auto workers and formulated the following propositions:

—Workers favor earlier retirement in the automobile industry insofar as they feel they will be receiving enough retirement income.

—The problems of job attachment are not as great for older men as has been thought in the past.

—Retirement is developing a positive image in the minds of these workers and is more of an anticipated feature of the life-cycle; it is seen as normal and good and not as a disruption of one's life.

—A general climate is also developing in which retirement is viewed positively by others close to the worker: family, friends, or co-workers.

—One of the main reasons for working as long as possible involves the problem of obtaining sufficient retirement income.

The exact nature of the impact of sex differences on the decision to retire is not known. Palmore (1965) found that: women retire more often than men; women retire for voluntary reasons more often than men; women show few occupational differences in retirement rates as compared with substantial differences among men; married women retire more often than unmarried women while married men retire *less* often than unmarried men; and retirement is increasing among men but not among women. However, the explanation for these patterns is unclear.

Using as a starting point the common stereotypes that most women do not work, and that work is of secondary importance to most working women, Palmore (1965:7-8) drew several conclusions. Women retire more frequently because it does not mean giving up a primary role. Because work is less important to women, they show little occupational variation in retirement rates. Married women can retire because their husbands can be expected to support them. Finally, because work is becoming less important for men, retirement is increasing, but this trend has had no impact on women.

As odious as these propositions might be to some, the use of sex in the assignment of roles is a reality in every society. There are many women who firmly believe that the women's role is in the home and who consequently never work at a paying job in their entire lifetime. However, in explaining the attitude toward retirement, of women who do work, Palmore ignores several alternatives. While it is no doubt true that some women who work do so purely for an added income, there are many women for whom being good at their work is very important. In a study of women teachers and telephone company employees, we found that a large proportion of the women in both occupations listed being good at their work as one of the three most important values of their lives (Cottrell and Atchley, 1969).

Nonetheless, women do retire more often than men do. Why? Palmore thinks it is because their jobs are less important to them. I suspect that at least as important is the tendency for others to expect the woman to put the housewife role first. Because women typically marry men who are older than they are, many women are encouraged to retire early by husbands who are already retired. Also, husbands may pressure their wives to retire in order to devote full time to the housewife role. The fact that women have restricted job opportunities as a result of sex discrimination also means that employed women are concentrated in less desirable jobs. Even professional women rarely are given opportunities for high-level positions. Accordingly, the percentage of women with challenging and satisfying work is much lower than among men. In our study, the telephone company men were much more likely to see their jobs as satisfying than were the women. Among teachers, on the other hand, the women found their jobs slightly more satisfying than did the men. This suggests that the different distribution of occupations among women may have a significant impact on the differential retirement rates.

No one knows how fast or how far the current trend toward sexual equality will go. This trend will undoubtedly influence the patterns of decisions to retire. At present, the retirement rates for men and women are converging. Nevertheless, much more research is needed on the mechanisms operating on the decision to retire among both men and women.

Summary

How an individual decides whether or not to retire is a complicated matter. To begin with, rules concerning retirement may be part of the job. These rules normally stipulate a minimum years of required service, a minimum age to qualify for retirement, and they often stipulate a maximum age at which the individual *must* retire. Most persons thus have an interval before the mandatory retirement age within which they themselves can control the timing of their retirement.

Each person must work his own desires around the constraints of his job. He cannot retire early unless he has met the minimum service and age requirements. Nor can he continue to work at a given job after the mandatory retirement age. Of course, someone who is forced out by mandatory retirement could theoretically get another job, but age discrimination makes securing a job difficult in later life.

The issue of the mandatory retirement age is not a simple one. On the one hand, mandatory retirement encroaches on the individual's right to work (an important value in many industrial societies). It sometimes wastes talent and produces financial hardship. On the other hand, mandatory retirement promotes planning for retirement. It also allows the individual to leave his job without ever having to face the question of whether he can still do the job adequately. Mandatory retirement reduces the possibilities for bias and favoritism in the determination of who is fit to stay on the job and who must go. Finally, it creates opportunities for advancement for younger workers. On balance, however, mandatory retirement policies are difficult to support with solid evidence, and the issue of mandatory retirement remains a controversial one.

Insofar as the individual *has* a choice concerning his retirement, there are a great many factors which may influence this choice. The attitudes of the individual himself toward retirement and toward leaving his job are important. Also important are the attitudes of his fellow workers, friends, and family toward his retiring. The prospect of financial hardship and the fear of free time are prime deterrents to retirement, while sufficient income, poor health, preretirement planning, and desire for leisure are major factors which promote retirement. Being married promotes retirement among women but works in the opposite direction among men. Women generally retire more frequently than men do. Age itself is an important correlate of the decision to retire but probably mainly because age is the criterion used to assign people to the retirement role.

Although we do not yet know exactly why, women are more likely to retire than men, and more often retire for voluntary reasons. Among women, there is little difference in retirement rates according to occupation, but much difference among men and retirement is increasing among men but not among women. The trend toward equality in occupational opportunity should serve to reduce these sex differences in future retirement rates.

5 • Retirement as an Event

Viewed as an event, retirement is what occurs at the precise point the individual leaves his job and is defined by himself, his employer, and others as having retired. The retirement event offers a rich field for study, but as yet it is relatively untouched.

Retirement as a Rite of Passage

Rites of passage are ceremonies that mark a critical transition in the life of a person from one phase to another. These ceremonies provide a standardized means of withdrawing from one social position to start another. Rites of passage are designed to help the individual define and accept his new position and to indicate formally to people around him that he has changed positions. For instance, the traditional marriage ceremony is a particularly elaborate and formalized rite of passage which is rich in the symbolism of changing social position. Thus, according to tradition, when the father of the bride passes her hand to the groom, this signifies the transfer of responsibility for looking after the woman from the father to the husband.

Van Gennep (1960) analyzed rites of passage in terms of three kinds of activities: activities symbolizing separation from the old position, activities symbolizing an intermediary status between the old position and the new, and activities symbolizing acquisition of the new position. Van Gennep also held that these three types of activities would vary in emphasis according to the type of transition. For example, separation is emphasized in funeral rites, the transitional aspect is often emphasized in initiation rites, and acquisition of the new position is emphasized in rites of coronation. Of course, all three could occur in any given rite of passage.

Retirement appears to be a case in which separation is the point of emphasis. In the typical retirement ceremony (at least as far as we know what is typical), there is simply a celebration of the past achievements of the job-holder and expressions of gratitude (often accompanied by some sort of momento). Almost never is the individual ceremonially prepared to take his new role, nor is there any ceremonial recognition or specification of the opportunities or responsibilities a person may expect in retirement. Of course, in order to prepare someone for a new position, it is necessary to have an idea of just what his opportunities and responsibilities will be. The fact that retirement ceremonies emphasize what the worker is retiring *from*, but have almost nothing to say about what he is retiring *to*, is probably a holdover from the widely held view that retirement represents neither opportunities nor responsibilities. As we shall see later, this view is not accurate, since there are definite rights and duties connected with retirement. However, as yet, few ceremonies incorporate these elements.

The tendency in retirement ceremonies to emphasize the separation aspects of the role change that occurs at retirement has the general result of making retirement ceremonies unhappy occasions, despite the veneer of smiles and handshakes. In the marriage ceremony, the bride's mother is told, "You're not losing a daughter, you're gaining a son." But in the retirement ceremony, the worker is told, "You're not losing your job, you're gaining nothing!" In fact, the worker is not passing into nothingness at retirement, but there is little in the typical retirement ceremony to reassure him.

As we shall see later, there are some good reasons why a very specific role definition for retirement is not necessarily possible or desirable. Nevertheless, there are some facets of retirement that *can* be specified, and these could be used to make the retirement ceremony less of an apparently negative event. For example, because retirement offers by definition an income free from job responsibilities, the individual has a greater opportunity to make his own decisions about the use of his time and talents. At the same time, this freedom might carry along with it a responsibility for public service beyond that which can be expected from those who hold full-time jobs. It could also be pointed out that retirement gives the individual the opportunity to exercise simultaneously two of the most highly prized qualities in the Western world—individualism and autonomy.

This type of positive thinking about retirement is kept out of retirement ceremonies probably because the people responsible for the ceremony have no notion of what the positive sides of retirement might be. While most people do have a positive attitude toward retirement, it is also usually a vague attitude. The lack of retirement education and the negative stereotypes about retirement combine to push people into simply avoiding the issue of the retirement role.

The negative nature of the retirement ceremony probably also accounts for the fact that such ceremonies are far from universal. Of course, many people retire under circumstances in which a retirement ceremony is not feasible. For example, retirement for some people means losing a job and not being able to find another. Also, retirement may be too gradual to single out the point at which a ceremony would be appropriate. Some employers doubtless avoid retirement ceremonies to escape drawing attention to how little they do toward giving their employees a financially secure retirement.

The social position of the individual who is retiring probably influences the likelihood that a retirement ceremony will take place and what it will consist of. For example, retiring professors who are well known in their fields are often given an impressive send-off with speeches, academic papers, and perhaps even a book of tributes to the work of the Great Man. These ceremonies can take as much as two or three days and draw colleagues and friends from a great distance. For the lesser-known professors and administrators, a faculty tea will usually do, and it is not uncommon to see several people being dispatched at one of these affairs. Finally, Old Charlie in the maintenance department is made the subject of a special coffee break, at which all of his co-workers look at their shoes while the boss tries to remember exactly what it was that Charlie did around there for all those years.

Obviously, one of the difficulties with a ceremony that stresses separation and gratitude for past accomplishments is what to do with people whose work was not particularly distinguished or whose jobs, though probably highly necessary, were not highly valued. At least a more balanced rite of passage could always say, "Now you are starting a new life."

It is also probable, given the current differentiation between the sexes in the job market, that women are less likely to experience a retirement ceremony. This might occur both because of the nature of "women's" jobs and because of the widespread belief that retirement is less meaningful to women. But even within the same occupation, women could be expected to experience a more positive type of ceremony because the housewife role gives people a concrete idea of what the woman is retiring *to*. Also, women have generally long since learned to accept unpaid volunteer service as a valid source of self-satisfaction.

In summary, only a minority of people experience this rite of passage, a retirement ceremony. For those women who do, it is probably a more positive event than for men, but for all who retire it is usually a ceremony which emphasizes separation from the job and which does very little looking forward.

The Last Day on the Job

Many people who do not experience a retirement ceremony do experience that "last day on the job." As yet, we know nothing about what sort of day this is for the people who experience it, or for their fellow workers. I would expect that the tone of the last day on the job would depend mainly on how the retiring worker feels about retirement and on how his fellow workers view it.

Activities on the last day probably range from normal work activities to a complete holiday, depending on the nature of the job, the prestige of the retiring worker, and probably a host of other factors.

Meanings that are exchanged on that last day also need study. What words are exchanged between the retirer and his fellow workers? Do the gestures employed reflect avoidance, reassurance, envy? Is there evidence of changes in the prestige, honor, or repute of the retirer in relation to others? Do others act in a manner that is envious, pitying, patronizing, concerned, happy, resentful, disinterested?

Retirement Gifts

Whether there is a retirement ceremony or not, the person who retires is often presented with a gift on his last day at the job. There are many types of gifts given on these occasions, ranging from cash gifts to personalized momentos to the standard "gold watch" type of gift.

We know very little about the role such gifts play in the retirement process. It is probably safe to say, however, that these gifts are intended to symbolize gratitude. What they in fact symbolize is problematic. To the retiring stock clerk who is facing a significant drop in income, cash gifts might be appreciated, especially if all of his fellow workers have "chipped in." To a retiring executive, however, a cash gift would probably be offensive, especially if people in the office "chipped in." Sometimes gifts can emphasize a desire for continued association between an organization and a retirer as in the case of employees who receive life-time passes to company recreational areas.[1] The standardized retirement gift is probably the most apt to be seen as a negative symbol to the retirer. Such gifts cannot help but be cold and impersonal symbols of the retirer's new status and, as such, their meaning again depends mostly on the retirer's attitude toward retirement.

Retirement Symbolism

A social symbol is a sound, object, event, word, gesture or action which has a socially defined meaning apart from its observable characteristics. Among other uses, symbols indicate the social position of an individual as a wedding ring symbolizes the fact that the wearer is someone's spouse. What symbols connect an individual with the retirement role?

Actually, the symbolism of retirement can begin some time before retirement. For example, entry into a preretirement counseling program by an individual and his or her spouse can symbolize the beginning of the retirement process. It can also set him apart from his fellow workers and cause him to enter a marginal position in which he is accepted neither as a full-fledged worker nor as a retired worker. At this point, participation in the preretirement program may become a symbol of transition.

There is also sometimes an attitude which symbolizes a person's impending retirement. In the armed services, an individual who is close to his time of discharge is allowed, with some ambivalence on both sides, to exhibit a "short-timer's attitude." This means that since the individual has only a short time to go on the job, he no longer has to play the worker role as strictly as he may have earlier when job security and promotions were serious concerns. The short-timer slides by with a minimal role performance, and takes his work much less seriously than he did earlier. In some ways this no doubt helps the individual to sever his psychological attachment to his job. Manifestations of a short-timer's attitude often identify the individual about to retire.

Sometimes the worker must train his own replacement. There is surely no act which could symbolize the reality of leaving one's job more than spending each working day training another person to take one's place.

Thus, there are many gestures, attitudes, and activities that symbolically label an individual and force him to acknowledge the reality of retirement. Retirement ceremonies and gifts also serve to label the individual as retired. Of course, retirement ceremonies and gifts symbolize the actual point of departure from the job, but for some workers the first symbol of retirement is their first pension check. Not going to work can seem like a vacation until that first pension check comes. Then the retirement event is symbolically complete.

In mass societies it is not possible to use personal characteristics to symbolize who a person is or what positions he holds. Instead, we use a complex and subtle system of clues, including style of hair and clothing, speech patterns, place of residence, and numerous others, to help us respond in appropriate ways to the strangers we inevitably encounter. What symbolizes a retired person? To begin with, there is no uniform, badge, or other insignia which we can use. There is no form of address peculiar to retired people. Only a tiny minority of retired people live in neighborhoods or communities that would automatically identify them as being retired. Retired people are often old and they often do not continue to live the nine-to-five life of a job holder but in this they are indistinguishable from the disabled or the unemployed. In fact, one is very hard put to discover any symbol that would identify most retired people. This lack of general symbolic identification for retirement status could be taken as evidence that the retirement role is less important to symbolize than other social roles the retired person may fulfill. Of course, an alternative explanation could be that as the retirement role becomes more institutionalized, symbols of retirement will appear.

Summary

Most of this chapter is speculation concerning the activities and symbols which make up the retirement event. Much research is needed in this area.

The retirement event can be a rite of passage in which there is a ceremony and often some sort of commemorative gift. However, this is not typical, and even when there is a ceremony, it tends to emphasize separation from the job with little concern for the future.

The last day on the job is a significant aspect of the retirement event, and what takes place on this day probably depends on several factors including the attitudes of the retirer and his fellow workers toward retirement, the type of job, and the prestige of the retirer.

Retirement gifts are intended as symbols of gratitude, but what they actually symbolize to the retirer depends on the type of gift and its relationship to the situation and needs of the retirer. Probably some gifts are appreciated and others are not, less in regard to what they are, than to how the retirer feels about retiring.

There are several factors which symbolically identify a worker as one about to retire and, therefore, perhaps a marginal man standing somewhere between full-fledged worker status and retired status. These include participation in preretirement programs, the "short-timer's" attitude, and having to train one's own replacement. However, as yet there are no common symbols which set the retired person apart from others in the larger community.

6 • Retirement as a Social Role

It has been customary for sociologists to refer to retirement as a "roleless role" (Donahue, Orbach, and Pollak, 1960; Burgess, 1960). This somewhat contradictory expression refers to the popular notion that retirement is a position in society for which there are no corresponding rights and duties in the culture. As Burgess put it,

> In short, the retired man and his wife are imprisoned in a roleless role. They have no vital function to perform . . . This roleless role is thrust upon the older person at retirement and to a greater or lesser degree he has accepted it or become resigned to it (1960:20).

This simplistic view is incorrect, and on more than one level. Part of the problem comes from a confusion over the definition of *role*. First, *role* can refer to the culturally transmitted, general norms governing the rights and duties associated with a position in society (judge, woman, retired person, mother, etc.). The rights of a retired person include the right to economic support without holding a job (and without the stigma of being regarded as dependent on society as in the case of the unemployed), the right to autonomy concerning the management of one's time, and often more specific rights such as the right to use company or union facilities, to hold union office, to retain various privileges and so forth.

Concerning retirement duties, Burgess and those with a similar view have made a serious mistake. Burgess speaks of giving up one's "vital function." This is an obvious reference to the fact that job roles usually exist in a context of interdependent tasks, each of which is necessary to the operation of the system. Yet job roles are always more than merely instrumental tasks. To a greater or lesser degree, they also include mannerisms, ways of thinking, and generalized skills which the individual often incorporates as part of himself. He is expected by others around him to continue to be the same type of person after retirement as he was before. Expected continuity of behaviour is a major set of expectations facing the retired person.

In addition, the retired person is confronted with other general duties. The most universal and important of these is the expectation that the retired person will assume responsibility for managing his own life. For a great many job-holders it becomes customary to let the employer decide how much insurance is adequate, when to get up in the morning, when to go on a trip, what kind of clothes to wear, and even what to do for recreation. For a great many people, job-holding means following the rules, not only on the job but in other areas of life as well. For these people retirement means a great deal of added decision-making responsibility. This means also that part of the time formerly devoted to the job must be set aside for these new decision-making duties. Also, regardless of the level of retirement income, retired people are expected to live within that income, another reason that not all of the time of the retired person is available for leisure. For even the most responsible and autonomous job-holder, retirement forces an increase in decision-making about his *personal* life.

In these and many other areas of life, retired people are expected to manage their own affairs without assistance. Put another way, retired people are expected to avoid becoming dependent either on their families or on the community. And just as income without job-holding is a reward for retirement, denegration is a punishment for those retired people who become dependent. Some might say that this proscription on becoming dependent is a facet of aging and not of retirement, but consider the difference in reaction to the dependency of a fifty-five-year-old retired man as opposed to the reaction to the same dependency of an eighty-year-old retired man. We expect the retired man to fend for himself, but we allow the old man more dependency.

Role can also be defined as a *relationship* between a particular position holder and other position holders. In this framework, the retirement role is the relationship between the retired
person and those who are still employed, either in a particular
profession on in a particular organization. The crux of the
relationship is the fact that both retired persons and the persons
still on the job tend to identify themselves in terms of the same
job or work organization. In this sense the position of retired
person is similar to the position of alumnus. As with alumni
of a given school, people recently retired from a job may be
envied by those they left still on the job, and interaction centers
around shared past experiences. However, the longer the elapsed
time in the retirement role, the fewer the number of "old buddies"
still on the job, and the relationship becomes characterized less
in terms of shared past experience and more in terms of abstract
notions of identity and loyalty. Loyalty to one's occupation,
employer, or colleagues is an important aspect of retirement
which has been the subject of too little research. The research
literature indicates that contacts between retired people and
those still on the job are not constant, but they are frequent
enough that most retired people gain some experience with
this particular aspect of the retirement role.

Thus, retirement does represent a role. However, the retirement role is usually defined in flexible, qualitative terms,
whereas job roles are more often expressed in concrete, instrumental terms.[1] It was probably the absence of the instrumental
element in job roles that led many investigators to view retirement as a "roleless role" and as an inevitable problem for the
retired person. These people saw retirement as creating a gap
which only a new instrumental or "functional" role could fill.
Much of the retirement literature still contains discussions
of possible functional alternatives to work (Miller, 1965).

However, other work (Schneider, 1964; Atchley, 1972; Streib
and Schneider, 1971) indicates that instrumental norms may
never need to develop around retirement. Schneider (1964)
makes the point well.

A clearly-defined role facilitates activity and gives a sense
of security to a person involved in a network of impersonal
universalistically-oriented judgments and evaluations. This
may not be the kind of world in which many older people

live. In the later years of life, the important persons in one's life—friends and relatives—know who the older person is and, therefore, he moves in a world that is familiar to him, and with which he is familiar. He may not need a sharply defined extra-familial "role" to give him an identity or to facilitate his own activity in his everyday world. We suggest, therefore, that so far as the older person himself is concerned, his willingness to leave the work force and perhaps his satisfaction with other aspects of life are not dependent upon whether he has a clearly defined alternative role or not. (Schneider, 1964:56)

Following this rationale, the retirement role, by its very vagueness, allows the individual a certain amount of flexibility in adjusting to his less consistent physical capabilities.

At this time, our ability to discuss the importance of social roles in later life is hampered by the lack of research and theory concerning the dynamics of role relationships in later life. Little attention has been paid to the impact of habit or reminiscence on the way people perceive their own performance of a role. There has been little examination of the effect of aging on the significance of fantasy in the role-taking process. And this work needs to be done, for until it is, our knowledge concerning re tirement as a social role will remain incomplete indeed.

Phases of Retirement[2]

When retirement is viewed as a social role, it is useful also to consider the various phases through which the role is approached, taken and relinquished. Yet because retirement has only very recently come to be viewed as a social role by sociologists, there has been little research on its phases. Accordingly, what follows is an attempt to sketch out the phases as we now know them, with the understanding that our knowledge is quite tentative in this area. Figure 2 gives an overview of the phases of retirement.

Preretirement

The preludes to retirement were discussed in Chapter 3. The preretirement period may be divided into two phases: remote and near. In the remote phase, retirement is defined by the

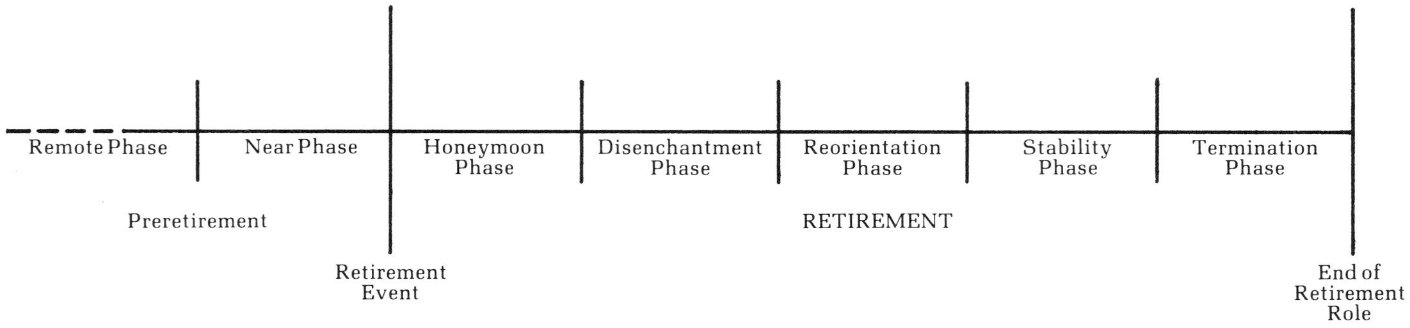

Figure 2. Phases of Retirement

Remote Phase | Near Phase | Honeymoon Phase | Disenchantment Phase | Reorientation Phase | Stability Phase | Termination Phase

Preretirement

Retirement Event

RETIREMENT

End of Retirement Role

individual as a vaguely positive phase of the occupational career which is a reasonable distance into the future. This phase can begin even before the individual takes his first job. It ends when the individual nears retirement. Even in the remote phase, most people expect to retire. Very few expect to die before they reach retirement age and very few expect to continue working until they die. Few people dread retirement at this point. At the same time, few people see retirement as requiring rational planning. Information-gathering concerning retirement tends to be unsystematic and only rarely intentional. The exceptions to this are those whose employers expose them to some sort of formal program during the remote phase, but such programs are very rare. Thus, anticipatory socialization for retirement in the remote phase tends to be informal and unsystematic. It may include positive attitudes and beliefs gained through experience. It may also include exposure to negative stereotypes concerning retirement which have been carried over from an earlier period in the evolution of industrial culture. Because socialization in the remote phase is informal and unsystematic, the outcome is understandably unpredictable. It also leaves to chance several issues which must be dealt with if the individual is to satisfy the prerequisites for successfully taking up the retirement role.

Socialization is intended not only to teach people how to play a role but also to alert them to the prerequisites of it. Thus, high school not only prepares students for college by teaching them (hopefully) how to learn but it also provides students quite systematically with knowledge concerning the SAT scores necessary for entrance to various types of colleges, the high school grades necessary for college, the funds necessary to attend various colleges, and sources of scholarships and loans. Most high schools attempt to provide this information early enough that students will know the prerequisites in time to satisfy them.

The retirement role also has prerequisites. The most important of these is a retirement income adequate for the style of life one wants to adopt in retirement. Prospective students from New York City who want to attend Princeton University have to do more financial planning than students who want to attend the City University of New York, where tuition is free to city residents. Likewise, people who want to lead an expensive life style in retirement must do more financial planning than those whose preferred life style can be maintained on Social Security benefits. Financing college educations is expensive and is best accomplished through long-range planning. The same is true of retirement, only more so. In retirement, the outlay is considerably larger and the time required to accumulate the necessary resources is much longer. Most people require a supplement to whatever retirement pensions they receive in order to sustain their desired life style. But in order to provide for this supplement, the individual must be aware of the need during the remote phase of preretirement.

Developing leisure skills is another prerequisite of the retirement role. These skills can sometimes be learned in later phases of retirement, but the literature on learning suggests that developing a wide variety of leisure skills is easier to accomplish during the early years of the remote phase of preretirement. The same can be said of developing ties with organizations in the community.

Smooth adjustment to retirement is associated with financial security and personal adaptability. At present, very little systematic effort is devoted toward developing these characteristics during the remote phase of preretirement. And a good case can be made for the need of such efforts, especially among working-class people. Yet, as haphazard as the socialization for retirement is during the remote phase of preretirement, people in general are not totally unprepared for retirement, they are merely inadequately prepared.

The near phase of preretirement begins when the individual becomes aware that he will take up the retirement role very soon. This phase is often initiated by an employer's preretirement program. It may also be initiated by the retirement of slightly older friends. For women, it is often initiated by their husband's retirement. At this point, attitudes toward retirement become more negative.

Attitudes toward retirement generally become more negative during the near retirement phase probably because the realities of retirement become clearer and because so many individuals currently are faced with not having met the financial prerequisites for taking up the retirement role. Yet there are many who remain quite positively oriented toward retirement during this phase. Preretirement planning programs help to offset the negative stereotypes concerning retirement, and there are many whose financial outlook is quite good. The leisure skill issue is particularly of concern to working-class people during this phase.

Preretirement programs most often are offered to people in the near phase of preretirement. The range of topics varies, but financial planning and the use of leisure time are the two most common topics. These programs are successful in reassuring people and reducing their anxieties about retirement. But at this late stage it is usually impossible to remedy large deficiencies in preretirement socialization. It is especially difficult to do much about inadequate financial planning at this stage.

During the near phase, the individual begins to gear himself for separation from his job and the social situation within which he carried out that job. He may adopt a "short-timer's attitude." He may begin to notice subtle differences in how he is viewed by others around him. As we said earlier, whether the person nearing retirement gets positive or negative reactions depends on the prevalent view of retirement on the part of those with whom he interacts.

Participation in retirement planning programs, retirement ceremonies, presence of an on-the-job trainee for replacement, and sometimes "promotion" into a less essential job are all mechanisms which serve to publicly define a person as being in the near phase of preretirement. In a job situation where retirement is viewed negatively, the individual can be expected to avoid these symbolic indicators of status decline. In a job situation where retirement is viewed positively, individuals can be expected to welcome these symbolic indicators of a gain in status.

During the near phase of preretirement, the retirer, to the extent that he normally engages in fantasy, will develop a fairly detailed fantasy of what he thinks retirement will be like. These fantasies may be quite accurate pictures of the future or they may be totally unrealistic. There is always an element of idealization in fantasy, but there is also a great deal of difference between pragmatic idealism based on knowledge, and romantic idealism based on wishful thinking. To the extent that fantasy is realistic, it can serve as a "dry run" which may smooth the transition into retirement by identifying issues requiring advanced decision-making. To the extent that fantasy is unrealistic it may thwart a smooth transition into retirement by setting up a detailed but unrealistic set of expectations. At this point, we know very little about the details of retirement fantasy during the near phase of preretirement and the role it plays in retirement adjustment. This is yet another promising area for research.

The Honeymoon Phase

The retirement event is often followed by a rather euphoric period in which the individual wallows in his newfound freedom of time and space. It is in this phase that people try to "do all of the things I never had time for before." The honeymoon period tends to be a busy time, filled with hunting, fishing, card-playing, sewing, seeing the grandchildren (or greatgrandchildren) and traveling, all at the same time. A typical person in this phase says: "What do I do with my time? Why, I've never been so busy!" The person in the honeymoon period of retirement is often like a child in a room full of new toys. He flits from this to that, trying to experience everything at once.

Not everyone has a honeymoon, however. For one thing, not everyone can afford it. For others, field of choices is pretty limited—by finances, by life style, by health, by family situation, or any of a number of other constraints.

The honeymoon period of retirement may be quite short or it may extend for years, depending on the resources available to the individual and his imaginativeness in using them. However, most people find that they cannot keep up the frantic pace of the honeymoon period indefinitely, and they then settle into some sort of routine.

The nature of the routine which follows the honeymoon period is important. If the individual is able to settle into a routine that provides a satisfying life, then that routine will probably stabilize. Many people whose off-the-job lives were full prior to retirement are able to settle into a retirement routine fairly easily. For these people, choices among activities and groups were made earlier. All that remains is to realign one's time in relation to those choices.

The Disenchantment Phase[3]

However, for some people it is not easy to adjust to retirement. After the honeymoon is over and life begins to slow down, some people experience a period of let-down, disenchantment, or even depression. The depth of this emotional let-down is related to a number of factors. People with few alternatives, those who have little money or poor health, those who were over-involved in their jobs, those who are unaccustomed to running their own lives, those who experience other role losses in addition to retirement, those who leave communities where they had lived for many years—these are the people who are apt to experience deep and lengthy periods of depression following the honeymoon period.

In a sense, the honeymoon period represents a living out of the preretirement fantasy. The more unrealistic the preretirement fantasy turns out to have been, the more likely it is the retirer will experience a feeling of emptiness and disenchantment. Consequently, the failure of the fantasy represents the collapse of a structure of choices, and what is depressing is that the individual must start over again to restructure life in the retirement role. "So traveling constantly turned out to be a bore, now what?" This is the kind of question people face in the disenchantment phase.

In other cases, the disenchantment phase results from the failure of anticipatory socialization for retirement. Somehow the individual developed a concept of the retirement role that was either too unrealistic or too vague to be workable. Such failures are common. Quite often our fantasies of positions we are about to occupy are too unrealistic or vague to be workable, and we solve the problem by on-the-job training. Most people eventually work their way through the disenchantment phase, but some remain in this phase.

Because the bulk of the research is structured so as to measure people's reactions to retirement just before retirement, just after retirement, or all across the span of retirement, we have very little concrete data on the disenchantment phase of retirement. This would be an especially fruitful area for further longitudinal research.

The Reorientation Phase

A reorientation phase is necessary for those whose honeymoons either never got off the ground or landed with a loud crash. During the reorientation phase, the depressed person "pulls himself together." This process involves using one's experience as a retired person to develop a more realistic view of alternatives. It also involves exploring new avenues of involvement. Very few people elect to become hermits in retirement. Most want to remain involved with the world around them.

Groups in the community sometimes help people during the reorientation phase. For example, many people become involved in Senior Center activities for the first time during this phase. Outreach programs of community agencies and churches also sometimes help.

But for the most part, the individual is on his own during the reorientation phase, and if he seeks help it is most often from his family and close friends. The goal of the reorientation process is a set of realistic choices which can be used to establish a structure and a routine for life in retirement which will provide for at least a minimum of satisfaction. People playing the retirement role do not aim for ecstatic bliss. They are quite willing to settle for an existence that is satisfying at least some of the time. This sort of criterion is used in other roles much earlier in life; therefore, applying it is seldom a problem for retired people. Most people who enter the reorientation phase of retirement pass through it to a stability phase, but some never quite achieve the needed degree of reorientation.

The Stability Phase

Stability here refers not to the *absence* of change, but to the routinization of criteria for *dealing with* change. In the stability phase of retirement, the individual has a well-developed set of criteria for making choices, and these allow him to deal with life in a reasonably comfortable, orderly fashion. Life in the stability phase may be busy, and certainly it may have exciting moments, but for the most part it is predictable and satisfying. Many people pass into this phase directly from the honeymoon phase; others reach it only after a painful reassessment of personal goals; others never reach it. It is the ultimate phase in terms of role playing.

In the stability phase of retirement, the individual has mastered the retirement role. He knows what is expected of him, he knows what he has to work with—what his capabilities and limitations are. He is a self-sufficient adult, going his own way, managing his own affairs, bothering no one. Being retired is for him a serious responsibility, seriously carried out.

During the stability phase the individual inevitably encounters physical declines which change his level of functioning. But these changes too can usually be incorporated into the routine without changing the criteria for making choices. Sometimes, however, physical disabilities or losses of other roles are serious enough to cause a need for a new routine. At this point, the individual may regress back to the reorientation phase.

Termination Phase

Many older people die rather abruptly with no lengthy period of disabling illness. For these people, death may end the retirement role while they are still in the stability phase. But people can lose their retirement role in other ways. Most often, the retirement role is cancelled out by the illness and disability which sometimes accompany old age. When an individual is no longer capable of engaging in major activities such as housework, self-care, and the like, he is transferred from the retirement role to the sick and disabled role. This transfer is based on the loss of able-bodied status and the loss of independence, both of which are required for adequate playing of the retirement role. Another way that an individual may lose his retired status is to lose his financial support. At that point, he ceases to be retired and comes dependent. Of course, if he takes a full-time job, the individual loses his retired status.

The increasing dependence forced by old age usually comes gradually enough that the retirement role is given up in stages. Only upon institutionalization do independent choices begin to become so trivial as to totally remove the dignity inherent in the retirement role.

Timing of Phases

Because there is no universal point of retirement, there is no way to tie the phases of retirement to a chronological age or to a period of time. These phases refer rather to a typical progression of processes involved in approcahing, playing and giving up the retirement role. Any given individual may not experience all the phase or experience them in the order presented here.

Retirement vs. Other Roles

Retirement affects other roles in at least three ways. It increases the time available for playing other roles. It changes the economic wherewithal available for playing other roles. And it changes the manner and quality of other role-playing.

The increase in time results from the fact that the personal decision-making and management functions which make up the retirement role do not require all of the time freed by loss of the job. This is particularly true once the stability phase of retirement is reached. This increased involvement may be wanted by the role-set or it may not.[2] For example, some wives welcome their husband's increased time spent around the house. Others do not. As one woman put it: "I married my husband for better or worse, but not for lunch."

Retirement income often necessitates curtailment of expensive leisure pursuits such as golf, boating or travel. It may also limit continued participation in voluntary associations which require dues. It may force the family to relocate.

Probably most important is the change which occurs in the *quality* of other role-playing, especially in the family. One of the things retired men inevitably seem to do is to take more part in taking care of the household. Middle-class wives usually welcome this trend, but working-class wives often do not. In general, however, retirement generally increases marital satisfaction (Rollins and Feldman, 1970).

Summary

Retirement is not a void. It represents a valid social role which consists not only of rights and duties attached to a social position but also of specific relationships between retired people and other role players.

Like other roles, retirement involves a progression of processes through which the role is approached, played, and relinquished, and it interacts with other roles the indivudual plays.

Retired people are expected to remain the same type of person, to assume responsibility for managing their own lives, to avoid becoming dependent and to live within their incomes. Retired people receive pensions and various privileges. The relationships of retired people to their former work organization are similar to those of alumni to their school.

Socialization for retirement involves establishing prerequisites at least as much as it does developing specific knowledge or skills. This would ideally take place in the remote preretirement phase but it seldom does. In the near preretirement phase, the individual develops a detailed fantasy concerning retirement. In the honeymoon phase, he tries to live out that fantasy. If his fantasy is adequate, he moves into a stable phase typified by a detailed set of criteria for making routine choices and giving structure to retirement. To the extent that the fantasy is inadequate, the individual enters a disenchantment phase following the honeymoon. Eventually, he enters a reorientation phase in which a viable pattern for choice-making is sought. The termination phase of retirement is usually brought on by death or by a transfer to a sick and disabled role.

7 • Retirement Income

In Chapter One, part of the definition of retirement involved provision of income based on having held a job in the past. A retirement pension is a periodic allowance paid to someone because he had fulfilled the necessary age and length of service requirements. Of course, there are other types of pensions—disability, veterans, widows, etc.—but here we are concerned with retirement pensions.

Retired people also receive income from other sources, but not because they are retired. Public assistance is paid only to the old who are destitute and can prove it. Income from assets is available whether a person is retired or not. Thus, pensions are the only income source directly related to retirement. Yet in examining incomes in retirement it is also necessary to take a look at total income and the part that pensions play in the total incomes of retired people.

Pensions

Retirement pensions are of two main varieties: *general public pensions* which are available to everyone who has held a job, regardless of earnings, occupation, or employer, and which are administered by the national government; and *job-specific pensions* which are usually insurance-type pensions administered to former holders of specific jobs on behalf of a particular employer or union. The discussion of pensions which follows is based on the pension system in the United States, and the information is drawn primarily from the 1968 Survey of the Aged conducted by the Social Security Administration and from the annual statistics for 1970 (Social Security Administration, 1970).

74

Social Security

Social Security is the most common term used to denote the retirement pension received under the old-age insurance provisions of the Social Security Act. A person entering the labor force in 1952 or later must work at least ten years at a job covered by Social Security and reach at least age sixty-two in order to qualify for a pension.[1] Thus, Social Security is in fact a job-related pension based on fulfillment of age and length of service criteria.

The pension a worker receives under Social Security may also contain, in addition to the pension the worker himself has qualified for, a supplement for support of a spouse and/or children. If a worker dies, a reduced pension is available to his surviving spouse. This provision is often absent from job-specific pensions. For example, if a man is entitled, based on past earnings, to a monthly retirement pension of $200, then he and his spouse would be entitled to a family benefit of $300 per month. If the man dies and his wife is sixty-five or over, she is entitled to the full amount of her husband's benefit, in this case $200. If the widow remarries, she must revert to a spouse's benefit, 50 percent of the benefit of either her deceased husband or her present husband, and in most cases she will encounter a reduction in benefits. Thus, Social Security still financially penalizes widows for remarrying. If the marriage fails, the widow can revert back to her widow benefit from her deceased husband.

When the Social Security system was initiated in 1935, only workers in commerce and industry were covered. Gradually, other groups such as farm workers, members of the armed forces, and the self-employed were added to the pool of compulsory coverage. By 1968, virtually all job holders were covered. The only major exception was the provision that certain employees of state and local government could elect, by agreement of both employer and employees, to remain outside the Social Security system. Teachers in the State of Ohio, for example, are not covered by Social Security. However, Ohio teachers are covered by a compulsory pension system which provides to those who retire at age sixty-five or more with thirty years of service a pension equal to 90 percent of the individual's average annual income for the five years of highest income. Most public employees not covered by Social Security receive substantial pensions, but there is also a group of individuals at the bottom of the economic scale who have not accumulated enough work experience on a job covered by Social Security to qualify for even the minimum benefit.

As of 1967, nine out of ten couples or individual persons age sixty-five or over in the United States were receiving retirement pensions under Social Security. The one person in ten who did not receive benefits was, in most cases, entitled to Social Security but not collecting it because he was still working. Among single women over sixty-five, however, there were many who were neither working nor entitled to a Social Security pension. A great many of those older women who were drawing Social Security pensions were widows of workers.

In 1967, the amount of the Social Security pension claimed at age sixty-five by an individual ranged from $55 per month (the minimum benefit) to $218 per month. In terms of annual incomes, the median Social Security pension was $2,187 for married couples, $1,368 for single men, and $1,044 for single women.[2] Elsewhere (Atchley, 1972:140) I estimated that the bare minimum income requirement was as follows:

	Couples	Individuals
Own Home Free and Clear	$2,300	$1,720
Other	$2.660	$1,925[3]

Thus, income from Social Security pensions alone is clearly inadequate to meet needs for more than half of those receiving benefits. Recent increases in Social Security pension levels still leave a majority receiving pensions which do not meet even minimum needs.

As of 1972, the average annual retirement benefit was $3270 to couples, $2124 to single men, and $1682 to single women. Adjusting for changes in the value of the Dollar, this was the equivalent of $2190, $1423, and $1127 in 1967 Dollars. In other words, there was virtually no change in the purchasing power of Social Security retirement pensions from 1967 to 1972.

The group receiving the minimum pension ($660 per year in 1967, raised to $844.80 in 1971) is of particular interest. About 15 percent of all persons who receive retirement pensions from

Social Security receive the minimum. Of those who do receive the minimum, half are retired single women, a quarter are widows or retired single men, and the other quarter are retired married couples (Lauriat, 1970). Minimum benefits tend to go to those who had very low earnings, irregular employment, a short period of employment, or a combination of these characteristics. Drawing the minimum pension from Social Security is also related to having had little formal education, having had health problems which interfered with work, and having been a wage earner in a service or unskilled blue-collar occupation (Reno and Zuckert, 1971). For many of these people, the same factors which caused them to receive a low Social Security pension also prevented them from accumulating other kinds of resources which could be used in retirement (Lauriat, 1971). It should not be too surprising that a large proportion of those drawing the minimum Social Security pension still work to supplement their pensions.

Single women do not fare very well as Social Security pensioners. Because women are concentrated in jobs with low earnings, because their work careers are often interrupted for child-rearing, and because widows do not qualify for the full value of their deceased husbands' pensions, single women dominate the group receiving pensions far below the poverty line. Only women with professional or technical occupations escape high proportions receiving the minimum pension.

In general, widows who draw survivors benefits are better off than are single women who draw pensions based on their own earnings. Only 11 percent of the widows draw the minumum pension, while 28 percent of retired women workers draw the minimum. However, hidden in these statistics is a sizable group of widows who draw pensions based on their own earnings because their survivors benefits would have been even lower than the minimum pension.

Black workers also have Social Security pensions which reflect the effects of past job discrimination. A quarter of the men and a fifth of the women who draw the minimum benefit are black. In 1970, black workers, both men and women, averaged pensions about $250 per year below the average for whites. For all categories of pension recipients, blacks have pensions which are consistently about $20 per month lower than the pensions for whites in the same category.

In general, the older the individual, the lower the Social

Security pension. This results from the fact that while cost-of-living increases have been applied to ease the impact of inflation, little has been done to adjust for the overall increase in real income since 1935. Admittedly, cost-of-living increases partially take care of this problem, but even so, the average pension of new beneficiaries at age sixty-five was $1,771.92 in 1970 as compared with $1,073.40 during the same year for those age ninety-five or over. And this problem is compounded because extreme old age drastically increases the need to buy services.

Thus, while Social Security pensions have the virtue of being available to almost everyone, the level of income they provide is meager at best, and for many it is significantly below the amount of income necessary to provide even the barest essentials. As we shall see later, this is a very serious matter since nearly 80 percent of retired American households must rely entirely on their Social Security pensions.

In January, 1974, an important change took place in the Social Security system. At that time, a special "supplemental Social Security income payment" went into effect which guaranteed every older American $146 per month from Social Security regardless of prior work history. Obviously, this departs from the old concept of pensions based on prior service. For example, if an individual received a Social Security retirement pension of $110 per month as his only income under the old system, he now can exclude $20 of his pension income, giving him an effective pension income of $90 per month. This would entitle him to an additional $56 per month in supplemental benefits, and his total benefit amount would be $166 per month. Thus, for those receiving Social Security retirement pensions the guarantee is actually $166 per month, and only those who did not qualify for any job-based pension would receive the $146 per month minimum.

Despite the fact that the supplemental payment is available to everyone, regardless of prior work history, Social Security will probably continue to be regarded generally as a legitimate income source. However, should the supplemental provisions come to be viewed as welfare, then Social Security retirement pensions may decline in terms of social acceptability. This is an excellent subject for research, for the new provisions would put more people on an equal income level than have ever been before.

Job-Specific Pensions

Job-specific pensions come in two varieties: private group pensions from businesses or unions, and public pensions provided through government employers. In 1967, 77 percent of retired households in the United States received no pension other than Social Security. Three percent received a public pension and not Social Security; 7 percent received a public pension *and* a Social Security pension; 13 percent received a private group pension *and* a Social Security pension. From these data it is clear that job-specific pensions in the United States are designed to operate in conjunction with Social Security.

Private Pensions

Since most private pensions came along after the Social Security Act became law, it is not too surprising that private pensions are designed primarily as supplements to Social Security pensions. Private pensions currently provide meager supplementary income because those who are drawing the benefits generally had only a few years of coverage prior to retirement. However, as private pension systems begin to mature, the level of benefits they provide should improve. Kolodrubetz (1970:19) reports that from 1962 to 1967 the median private pension income for couples rose from $790 per year to $970.

Schulz (1970) indicates that increases in the proportion of workers covered by private pensions is likely to grow slowly due to the obstacles in securing coverage for these segments of the labor force not now covered. In addition, those covered by private pensions do not always collect them. First, the company or the union must operate long enough to fill up the retirement fund. Second, the individual cannot change jobs. Schulz (1970:39) quotes one source as saying: "In all too many cases, the pension promise shrinks to this: 'If you remain in good health and stay with the same company until you are sixty-five years old, and if the company is still in business, and if your department has not been abolished, and if you haven't been laid off for too long a period, and if there is enough money in the [pension] fund, and if that money has been prudently managed, you will get a pension.' " Schulz concludes that the inequities of private pensions often outweigh their virtues.

In 1974 Congress passed the Employee Retirement Income

Security Act aimed at solving some of the problems referred to above. It seeks to protect workers from losing their pension rights by placing Federal controls over vesting and financing of private pensions. An employee is "vested" at the point he or she is guaranteed a share of the employer's private pension fund. A vested individual is entitled to some benefits even if he or she leaves the organization prior to retirement age. The new law offers employers three options for vesting the pension rights of their employees.

> Option 1: Employees' accumulated benefits are 25 percent vested after 5 years, gradually increasing to 100 percent vested at the end of 15 years.
> Option 2: 100 percent vesting of accumulated benefits after 10 years, nothing before that.
> Option 3: 50 percent vesting when age and length of service combined equal 45, the remaining 50 percent vested within 5 years.

The new law also creates a Pension Benefit Guarantee Corporation under the Labor Department to protect workers covered by pension plans that fold. In addition, standards were established for financing and administering pension plans. If these standards are adhered to, then private pension funds should be more solvent than in the past.

While the Employee Retirement Income Security Act was landmark legislation, it was clearly a compromise which left several issues unresolved. First, there is no requirement that employers provide private pensions. Second, there are no provisions to guarantee portability of pension rights—the ability to take pension rights from one employer to another. Finally, the machinery for enforcing violations of the Act has yet to be tested.

Hurwitz and Burris (1972) found that from 1958 to 1969, nearly 10 percent of the pension plans covering United Auto Workers were terminated. They studied those plans which did terminate, and they found that generally those who were already retired continued to receive their pensions, but that most workers not yet retired lost most or all of their pension coverage. They conclude that large numbers of workers in the future will not receive the private pension they have come to expect. In addition, plant closings will result in the loss of fringe benefits such as health insurance as well as pensions.

Private group pensions are much less common than is generally thought. In some ways, private pensions have probably hurt the chances of raising Social Security pensions to a decent level. This is particularly unfortunate since private pensions tend to be concentrated in high-paying industries and occupations which produce high Social Security pensions as well.

Public Pensions

Three-fifths of those who receive public pensions but *not* Social Security are drawing pensions from Railroad Retirement. The rest are drawing some other form of government or military retirement. Public pensions of this type are considerably higher than both private pensions and Social Security pensions. In 1967, the median pension income for those receiving public pensions alone was $2, 720 for couples, $1, 995 for single men, and $1, 090 for single women (Kolodrubetz, 1970:9). This is substantially higher than the Social Security pension medians for couples and single men, but the figure for single women is about the same (Kolodrubetz, 1970:8).

For the 7 percent who receive a public pension *and* Social Security, the picture is even better since in this category couples average $1,800; single men $1,394; and single women $1,005, all receiving this money in addition to their Social Security pensions, (Kolodrubetz, 1970:9).

Public retirement programs tend to relate pensions to peak earnings and to contain automatic provisions for cost-of-living increases. Also, public employees in general have more orderly work histories which in turn entitles them to higher benefits. A third factor is the maturity of public pension plans in relation to private pensions. Public pension programs also typically involve high levels of employee contributions. All of these factors combine to make public pensions generally more adequate than private pensions.

Within the public sector, however, there are some wide variations, just as there are in the private sector. In Ohio in 1969, for example, the average pension for retired school employees was $1,188 per year as compared to an average of $4,152 for retired highway patrolmen (Atchley, et al., 1972:20).

Dual Pensions

In 1967, 20 percent of the retired households in the United States were receiving two pensions, a Social Security pension plus either a private group pension or a public pension. These people enjoyed retirement incomes well above the level required to meet minimum needs. The average was more than $4,300 for couples in this category, over $2,700 for single men, and over $2,300 for single women. The only category of single women with an average pension even at, much less over, the bare minimum was single women with dual pensions.

Dual pensions serve to widen the gap between the haves and the have-nots in terms of pension incomes because second pensions are concentrated among high-paying employers and occupations. The higher earnings, which make a second pension possible, also result in high Social Security pensions. Persons with private pensions are particularly likely to have high Social Security pensions. Dual pensioners thus average combined pensions twice as high as the average for persons with Social Security pensions alone.

Assets

Saving money for use in one's old age is a time-honored tradition. Yet few people live up to the ideal in any substantial way. About half of the retired population has income from assets, but the level of asset income is generally low. In fact, most retired people have liquid assets of $2,000 or less. Depending on the form of investment, $2,000 will yield no more than around $160 per year, hardly substantial supplement to pension income. Those with enough liquid assets to provide substantial incomes tended to be the same people who enjoyed substantial pensions (Murray, 1972). Only a tiny proportion have incomes from private annuities.

About 60 percent of retired couples own their homes free and clear as compared with only about 30 percent of retired single people. This is the most common financial asset of retired people, and it is widely thought that home ownership drastically cuts income requirements. But it has been estimated that home ownership is worth at most $400 per year in terms of reducing income requirements (Atchley, 1972:140). In addition, home ownership is worth very little as a contingency reserve.

Earnings

About a million and a half couples drawing Social Security pensions in 1967 also reported part-time employment. Because the median incomes of pensioners who held jobs fell just short of the level among those who are fully retired with dual pensions, a case could be made that the primary motivation for staying on the job while drawing Social Security appears to be financial need.

Earnings are more likely to be part of the income picture of retired couples as compared with unmarried people. In 1967, 43 percent of the couples receiving Social Security reported earnings, while only 16 percent of unmarried people with Social Security pensions reported earnings. In terms of aggregate income, earnings accounted for 30 percent of the total income of couples receiving Social Security pensions, but only 12 percent of the total income for single individuals.

Given the fact that incomes of single people in retirement tend to fall far below the minimum requirement, one might expect a larger proportion to be employed. But the median age of retired, unmarried people is considerably higher than for retired couples, and the older the individual is, the less able he is to secure employment.

Cash Gifts

Cash gifts from family or friends not in the household were reported by only 3 percent of the retired, but among unmarried women the figure rose to 5 percent (Bixby, 1970:13). In terms of aggregate income, contributions from outside the household accounted for less than 1 percent of the income of retired people.

Public Assistance

Given the large number of retired people with no source of income other than a Social Security pension and the general inadequacy of these pensions, it is not surprising that nearly 100,000 people (about 8 percent) of Social Security recipients are also receiving public assistance. What is surprising is that the number is not larger, particularly among unmarried pensioners. Given the low level of pensions from Social Security, a large number of pensioners need supplementary income just to get up to the bare minimum. As we have seen, some people cope with this problem through earnings from employment.

But this strategy is possible for only about 20 percent. Eight percent receive public assistance. About 3 percent receive contributions from relatives. That still leaves a sizeable proportion with no source of the necessary supplement to their pensions. Most of these people do not seek public assistance because of pride. In American society, people who accept charity are looked down upon. A Social Security pension is seen as an earned right. Public assistance is seen as charity. The former is acceptable; the latter is not. Many retired people would literally starve before they would go through the demeaning ritual necessary to receive public assistance.

The Income Picture

Only about 10 percent of retired American households have annual incomes of $5,000 or more, and 65 percent have annual incomes under $3,000. Social Security retirement pensions are the sole source of income for nearly 80 percent of retired Americans. Two-thirds of retired Americans are trying to live on incomes at or below the minimum required to proved basic necessities.

Single women, widows, older retired people, and blacks are particularly likely to be drawing grossly inadequate pensions. Illness, irregular work history, or a low-paid occupation were factors which were also associated with drawing inadequate pensions. This problem is further compounded by the fact that these same categories of retired people are the least likely to have income from earnings, assets, or cash contributions from families. These groups are most likely to receive public assistance in addition to a Social Security pension.

Job-specific pensions are in themselves not particularly impressive, but most of these pensions are supplements to a Social Security pension, and the combined results of dual pensions yield modest but adequate incomes for retired people in this category. Table **6** shows clearly that in terms of total retirement income, those with dual pensions are indeed the elite. Unfortunately, only about 20 percent of retired households in America receive dual pensions.

People with high pension incomes predominate among those with high incomes from assets. Incomes from assets and pensions are highly correlated with one another primarily because they both tend to be based on the same factor—income level during the working years.

Table 6. Median Annual Total Income in 1967 of Retired Households, by Type of Pension Income.*

Sources of Retirement Benefit	Median Income		
	Married Couples	Nonmarried Men	Women
Social Security only	$2,752	$1,488	$1,195
Social Security *and*			
Private Pension	4,257	2,580	2,331
Public Pension	4,424	2,848	2,319
Public Pension only	3,746	-**	1,290

* Since this table deals with *total* income, it does not agree with data given earlier for *pension* income only.

** Not reported. However, pension income only for this group was $1,995.

Source: Kolodrubetz (1970:4)

From this is should be clear that while a small but highly visible minority of retired Americans has ample pensions, most are struggling to make ends meet. Social Security pensions are the primary source of retirement income in America, yet the level of these pensions is generally inadequate. Private group pensions, public pensions, earnings, and income from assets plug the gap for a few, but the vast majority are left to fend for themselves. The only recourse is to accept charity, either from the family or from the community, or to slowly let things deteriorate.

The income picture for the retired is not improving either. In the past ten years, liberal increases in pension levels have been wiped out by inflation. In addition, millions of retired people have watched the purchasing power of their retirement incomes decline from ample to barely adequate. Retired people are on fixed incomes, and as general levels of living increase and inflation erodes purchasing power, those who have been in retirement for ten or fifteen years find their financial resources greatly reduced, even with the so-called cost-of-living increases in pension levels.

America is rapidly approaching a crisis in retirement finance.

Retired people increasingly see their incomes as inadequate and expect them to become more so in the future (Peterson, 1972). Inadequate retirement income is likely to become an even more important political and economic issue in the next few years. There have been many answers proposed, but the need is clear. Retirement income needs to be raised soon.

8 • The Consequences of Retirement

Retirement changes the individual, and it changes his situation. It also has important consequences for society.

Personal Consequences

It is widely held that retirement has an adverse effect on health. In discussions with people who have not yet retired, I frequently hear tales of people who carefully planned for retirement only to become sick and die within six months after leaving their jobs. Everyone seems to know people for whom this was true.

However, the crucial question is whether people retire because they are sick or whether they are sick because they retire. If people retire because they are sick, then it should not be surprising that some of them die. The decisive test of the impact of retirement on health is health following retirement as compared to just preceding retirement. Based on their data from a large longitudinal study of people both before and after retirement, Streib and Schneider (1971) concluded that health declines are associated with age, but not with retirement. That is, retired people are no more likely to be sick than people their same age who are still on the job. In fact, unskilled workers showed a slight *improvement* in health following retirement. In my own research, I have yet to encounter an occupational group for which retirement is related to a decline in self-reported health. It is true that many people expect retirement to adversely affect health, but very few realize their expectations. However, the measures used to assess health thus far have been heavily dependent on self-reporting of gross health changes.

Hopefully future longitudinal studies will make use of more sensitive measures of health. Until then, the research findings concerning the impact of retirement on health should be approached with caution.

While the general trends very definitely contradict the myth that retirement causes illness, there is nevertheless a small group of people who do become ill because of retirement. Ellison (1968) contends that much of the illness that does occur following retirement is a psychosomatic ploy used by the retired individual as justification for intruding on adult children and becoming dependent upon them. According to Ellison, these individuals view retirement negatively. They see retirement as robbing them of a place in society, and likewise, they see adopting the "sick role" as a way back into the system. Ellison expects this pattern to be most prevalent among the working class and among those who view retirement as a very uncertain position to be in. Ellison's work is not based on research evidence, however. What is needed is research on the extent to which illness and the sick role have and can be used by individuals who enter the disenchantment phase of retirement, discussed in Chapter Six, as a means of getting out of having to come up with a successful formula for playing the retirement role.

There has been a good deal of research devoted to the impact of retirement on mental disorders, but no definite impact has yet been found (Nadelson, 1969:11). Lowenthal (1964) found that mental illness tended to cause social isolation rather than the other way around. Likewise, it is quite probable that mental illness causes retirement rather than the other way around. However, there are several competing possibilities, none of which has yet been established. Several studies point to a higher incidence of mental impairment among retired people (Nadelson, 1969:10). However, Lowenthal and Berkman (1967: 76) found that the association between retirement and mental illness was mainly a function of poor health, low social activity, and unsatisfactory living arrangements rather than of retirement per se. They found that under conditions of relatively high socioeconomic status, retirement itself made little psychiatric difference. Other studies show no adverse effect of retirement on mental health (Nadelson, 1969:10). In my own research, I have seen cases in which retirement actually improved the level of functioning for people with psychiatric disorders. Job-related incidents often are precipitating factors in hospitalization for mental disorders. And to the extent that retirement removed the demand that the impaired individual cope with a complex and rigid role, then retirement tended to improve functioning.

A major portion of the literature on the personal consequences of retirement concerns the impact of retirement on social adjustment. The broad category of social adjustment includes such factors as acceptance of retirement, life satisfaction, morale, self-esteem, age identification, and job deprivation. It has been generally assumed that retirement has a negative impact on social adjustment, but as we shall see, this assumption is without basis in fact.

Streib and Schneider (1971:144) found that the percentage of retired people who said that retirement is good for a person increased substantially for each reporting period following retirement. This means not only that actual retirement increases the acceptance of retirement as a good thing, but also that the more experience people have with retirement the more likely they are to view it as a good thing. In our study of over 3500 retired teachers and telephone company employees, we found that 83 percent liked retirement. Of those who liked retirement, 20 percent reported anticipating that they wouldn't. The pattern of high acceptance of retirement prevailed regardless of sex or occupation (Cottrell and Atchley, 1969).

In their cross-national research, Shanas and her associates (1968:331) found that among their national samples of older men, there were major differences in the degree of acceptance of retirement. They found that Americans were much more accepting of retirement than Danes or Britains. In their U. S. sample, white-collar workers showed the greatest degree of acceptance of retirement, followed by blue-collar and service workers. American farmers were very likely to have a negative attitude toward retirement and were more similar to the Danes than to their fellow Americans in this respect. Half of the Danes in all classes rejected retirement outright as compared with 42 percent of the British men and 35 percent of the American men. However, based on the results of other studies, it appears that their American sample may overrepresent the percentage of Americans who reject retirement.

Morale and life satisfaction are two concepts which have

been used to identify a general construct having to do with an over-all emotional reaction to one's life at a given point in time. For example, Simpson, Back, and McKinney (1966:52) used the following scale and labelled it "morale."

> On the whole, I am satisfied with my way of life today.
>   (Strongly agree, agree)*
> As I get older, things seem to get better than I thought would be the case.
>   (Strongly agree, agree)
> I often feel that there is no point in living.
>   (Strongly disagree)
> Things just keep getting worse and worse for me as I get older.
>   (Strongly disagree)
> All in all, I find a great deal of unhappiness in life today.
>   (Strongly disagree)

They found that morale was generally unconnected to work or retirement. They concluded that morale is influenced as much or more by health, family situations, and other personal factors than by work or retirement. For example, Kerckhoff (1966:192), using the same data, found that high morale was associated with independence between generations in the family and with a functional home-based pattern of activities within the older couple. The only work related factor associated with morale was the tendency for those with orderly work histories to have high morale in retirement (Simpson, Back, and McKinney, 1966:67).

Streib and Schneider (1971:108) used the following measure which they called "life satisfaction:"

> In general, how would you say you feel most of the time—in good spirits or in low spirits?
>   (Usually in good spirits)
> How often do you find yourself feeling "blue"?
>   (Hardly ever or never)
> On the whole, how satisfied would you say you are with your way of life today?
>   (Very satisfied)

They found that retirement produced no significant change in life satisfaction. Nearly half of their respondents did not expect retirement to reduce life satisfaction, but even so a sizable proportion overestimated the adverse effect of retirement on life satisfaction (Ibid.:116).

In our study (Cottrell and Atchley, 1969:28) we used the following scale to measure "depression:"

> On the whole, how happy would you say you are?
>   (Not very happy, very unhappy)
> On the whole, I think I am quite a happy person.
>   (Disagree)
> In general, how would you say you feel most of the time—in good spirits or in low spirits?
>   (Neither good nor low spirits, fairly low spirits, very low spirits)
> I get a lot of fun out of life.
>   (Disagree)
> I wish I could be as happy as others seem to be.
>   (Agree)
> How often do you feel downcast and dejected?
>   (Very often, fairly often, occasionally)

Obviously, we were looking at the opposite end of the same scale used by Streib and Schneider—at the end which might be called "life dissatisfaction." We found that depression was uncommon among all of our subsamples. No category showed as much as 10 percent with a high degree of depression. However, women were significantly less likely to show a low degree of depression (72 percent) as compared to men (80 percent) and this was particularly true among the teachers. In all categories, however, over 70 percent showed a low degree of depression.

Apparently, however the subjective reactions to the retirement life situation are measured, retirement makes little difference, and the proportion with a high degree of satisfaction depends more on factors such as family situation, job history, and other personal factors than on retirement per se.

Another area of interest concerns the self. The self is an abstraction used by sociologists and psychologists to refer to the collection of ideas an individual holds concerning his own body, mind, behavior, and appearance to other people. The self can be subdivided into three parts: the "self-concept," "self-esteem," and "self-ideal." *"Self-concept"* refers to the cognitive elements of the self. It represents what the individual "knows" about himself. He gets this knowledge both from his own sensory observations and from the feedback he receives from others. *Self-esteem* refers to the emotional elements of the self, how the individual *feels* about himself. The norms of society provide the individual with a cultural ideal for personal qualities. The individual combines the cultural ideal with his own experience to develop a set of goals for the self called the self-ideal. Self-esteem is the product of a comparison by the individual of what he is (self-concept) with what he feels he ought to be (self-ideal) (Rosenberg, 1964).

Several aspects of the impact of retirement on the self have been studied. Back and Guptill (1966) used a semantic differential to study the self-concept among pre-retirees and retirees. They identified three dimensions: involvement, optimism, and autonomy. They found that the involvement scores for retired people were considerably lower than for pre-retirees. And this was true regardless of socioeconomic characteristics. However, retirement had very little effect on the optimism or autonomy dimensions (Ibid.:124). Back and Guptill conclude that the decline in perception of self as involved results almost entirely from loss of work. Their findings indicate that if the individual was healthy, had a middle or upper-stratum occupation, and had a high number of personal interests, then the loss of a sense of involvement brought on by retirement would be minimized. Nevertheless, they also conclude that even these retirees did not successfully fill the gap left by the loss of their jobs (Ibid.:129).

I studied the impact of retirement on self-esteem. Using Rosenberg's (1964) scale of self-esteem on our sample of retired teachers and telephone company employees (Cottrell and Atchley, 1969), I found that self-esteem in retirement tends to be quite high, much higher than among the high school students studied by Rosenberg (1964). I also found that retirement produced no differences in self-esteem scores.

Age identification is the individual's self-rating concerning his own phase of the life cycle. For example, Streib and Schneider (1971:97) used the following question:

Do you consider yourself:
_____ middle-aged
_____ late middle-aged
_____ old
_____ elderly

They found that a majority of their sample said, before retirement, that retirement would make no difference in age identification. An even larger percentage (70 percent) reported after retirement that retirement had made no difference in age identification. They conclude that chronological age rather than retirement is the primary factor in age identification.

We also studied the correlates of age identification (Atchley and George, 1973). The scale we used was slightly different.

In your view, which of the following best describes you?

_____ middle-aged
_____ just past middle age
_____ old
_____ very old

We found that the prime correlates of age identification as old or very old were retirement for men and chronological age for women. We concluded that men judged themselves in functional terms while women tended to judge themselves in more physical terms. Thus, for men our findings seem to disagree with those of Streib and Schneider.

The reason for this disagreement is probably more arbitrary than real. Streib and Schneider lumped late middle-aged, old, and elderly together into a category called "older." Our older category was made up of those who rated themselves as old or very old. Streib and Schneider's results thus refer to those who identify themselves as middle-aged vs. other, and retirement apparently has little effect on this. Our findings are more concerned with those who identify themselves as old as opposed to middle-aged. Retirement does make a difference for men.

The problem of reconciling our data with that of Streib and Schneider raises an important issue. There is a tendency for investigators to report their findings in terms of the constructs they are attempting to measure. Accordingly, Streib and Schneider discuss their findings as if the answer to their questions, coded the way they coded them, *were* age identification, instead of being merely a *measure* of age identification.[1] This is quite common and usually causes little problem among scientists because the operational definitions used are also included in research reports. For the layman, however, it is all too easy to forget that our use of the construct "age identification" refers to the answers to a specific question which we *assume* measures the construct. Thus, when reviewing the results of any study, two questions are equally important: 1) Is the measure used a valid measure of the construct?, and 2) Are the results obtained from the measure coded in such a way as to be valid in relation to the construct? This second question is crucial, yet information is often lacking concerning how categories are combined in statistical or tabular analysis.

The impact of the loss of the job role on the self has been the subject of several studies. *Job deprivation* is a construct which refers to the extent to which an individual misses his job. It is generally measured by the following scale (Thompson, 1958:37).

> I often miss being with other people at work.
>   (Strongly agree, agree)
> I often miss the feeling of doing a good job.
>   (Strongly agree, agree)
> I often wish I could go back to work.
>   (Strongly agree, agree)
> I often worry about not having a job.
>   (Strongly agree, agree)

Using this scale on our sample of retired teachers and telephone company employees, (Cottrell and Atchley, 1969) I found that about 80 percent showed a low degree of job deprivation. Simpson, McKinney and Back (1966: 84-89) used the same scale and found that low job deprivation in retirement was related to having looked forward to retirement,[2] having achieved most of one's job-related ambitions, and having an adequate retirement income. My findings were essentially similar, and I also found that low job deprivation was related to good health. From these findings, it appears that job deprivation in retirement depends on how retirement compares with life on the job. If retirement is viewed in advance as a negative thing, if the individual has the feeling of job goals still unmet, if retirement income is inadequate, and if health is poor in retirement, then it should not be too surprising that the retired individual misses the "good old days" on the job. Given the low levels of retirement income, it is surprising that high job deprivation is not more prevalent than it is.

Streib and Schneider (1971:128) used the same scale to examine the impact of retirement on job deprivation. They used a stricter definition of low job deprivation,[3] and they found that the length of time in retirement was associated with an increase in the percentage with low job deprivation.

Thus, the percentage of retired people who miss their jobs is small, and it gets smaller the longer people have been retired. A positive pre-retirement attitude toward retirement is the best predictor of low job deprivation in retirement. The level of job deprivation is more a function of a comparison between work and retirement than it is of any ingrained "work ethic."

Feelings of usefulness represent another area of the self related to work. Streib and Schneider (1971:117-126) asked their respondents to answer the question: "How often do you get the feeling that your life today is not very useful?" They found that the percentage of persons who "often" or "sometimes" felt useless averaged around 12 percent during the preretirement period and 27 percent after retirement. They report a consistent and marked increase in the percent feeling useless following retirement, but at no point does the proportion feeling useless go much over a quarter. Putting it another way, in retirement over 70 percent of their respondents seldom or never felt useless.

Social participation is another area where retirement is widely thought to have an effect. Social participation is assumed to be tied to support from a job role, and loss of the job role presumably hinders participation. In our study of teachers and telephone company employees (Cottrell and Atchley, 1969: 21), we found that only 6 percent of our sample saw five people or less in a week, and over a third saw more than thirty people a week. Nearly half reported that retirement had made no change in their number of contacts with friends, and 30 percent reported that retirement had increased contacts with friends. Women were more likely than men to report no change in contacts with friends. Former telephone company employees were significantly more likely to report *less* contact with friends following retirement, but even for telephone employees, less than a third reported less contact with friends.

Three-fourths of our sample reported the same or more participation in organizations following retirement. Men teachers were significantly less likely to experience a loss of participation as compared to other categories. Finally, three-fourths of our sample felt lonely "hardly ever" or "not at all." These data indicate that retirement generally either produces no change or *increases* social participation. Only in a relatively small minority of cases does retirement produce a decrease in participation and the consequent loneliness and isolation. And if the effects of widowhood are controlled, the proportion in this category is substantially reduced. Rosenberg's (1970) data suggest, however, that retirement is more likely to produce social isolation among the working class.

Bengtson (1969) examined the level of role activity among retired teachers and factory workers in six national samples.[4] He found three basic patterns of activity in relation to roles in families, organizational settings, and informal settings. The modal or most prevalent pattern was typified by a high level of family activity, intermediate activity in informal settings, and low activity in organizational settings. This pattern was present among the Polish and Italian samples and among workers in the U. S., West Germany and Austria. Teachers in the U. S. and West Germany had a pattern in which activity was moderate to high and there was relatively little difference in activity level among the three areas (family, formal settings, and informal settings). Finally, the Dutch showed a pattern in which family activity was very high, activity in formal settings was considerably lower, and activity in informal settings was lowest. However, within the Dutch sample, the teachers showed much higher levels of activity in non-family settings than did the workers. Bengston's data indicate that there are indeed national differences in terms of what kinds of activities occupy people in retirement. The Dutch are especially unique for their lack of involvement with friends and neighbors in retirement. Yet there were trends which reflected occupational rather than national differences. For example, a low degree of involvement in organized settings was typical of retired factory workers in all five national samples.

Simpson, Back, and McKinney (1966: 63-74) measured involvement with a scale in which values were assigned for joining or dropping out of organizations, changing number of friends, and gaining or losing interests. Involvement in retirement was directly related to occupational status, with retired professionals having the highest degree of involvement, semi-skilled workers having the least involvement, and middle-status workers being in-between. In terms of loss of involvement, however, the retired professionals had the highest percentage with some loss of involvement (61 percent); next came the semi-skilled retirees (51 percent); and middle-status retirees had the lowest percentage with some loss of involvement (40 percent). In interpreting these findings, it is important to note that Simpson, Back, and McKinney used a very liberal measure of loss of involvement. If the individual showed a *net loss* of as much as a single interest or organizational membership, then he was classified as a "loser", so to speak. Given the fact that professionals are highly involved to begin with, their percentage experiencing some loss is not especially serious, especially since the mean loss score for the group was only 1.5. However, the semi-skilled workers are not highly involved to begin with; and, therefore, the half of this group that experienced a loss of involvement in retirement may encounter more difficulty as a result.

Simpson, Back, and McKinney go on to conclude that many of the patterns of involvement supported by the job persist. They found that having a higher status occupation and an orderly work career were as crucial for involvement in retirement as they are at earlier ages. They also concluded that if social involvement is not developed prior to retirement, it is unlikely to be initiated after retirement. Finally, they conclude that it is not retirement *per se* that is responsible for the lack of involvement among semi-skilled retirees and some middle-status workers but instead their work histories that had not allowed them to become integrated into society. They particularly stress the role of financial security in providing support for participation in society.

Most people continue to do in retirement the same kinds of things they did when they were working. About a third increase their level of non-job-related role activities to fill the gap left by retirement. About a fifth of my sample of retired teachers reported that managing their own financial and social affairs absorbed a surprisingly large part of the gap left by retirement (Atchley, 1967). As one woman put it: "Now that I'm retired, I no longer have any excuse for not answering letters or calling on sick friends. It sometimes takes me half-a-day to answer one letter."

About a fourth of the retired population experiences a decrease in activities. This is not always an unwelcome decrease, however. As one man said to me: "It's nice not to have to keep up the pace anymore." This quote points up to the fact that activity is a relative matter. To someone who was uninvolved prior to retirement, leaving the job can result in an increase in activities and still leave gaps of unfilled, unsatisfying time. On the other hand, to an overinvolved professional, retirement may reduce the net amount of activity but at the same time bring the level down to a point more suitable to the person's capabilities and desires.

A great deal of attention has been paid of the impact of retirement on *leisure participation*. According to one school, leisure is not something that can be legitimately done full-time by adults in Western societies without resulting in an identity crisis for the individual and a social stigma of implied inability to perform (Miller, 1965). I suspect that at one time, and in some cultures more than others, this set of assumptions was widely applicable. In fact, much of the retirement research done in the U. S. in the early fifties supports such a view. However, there is growing evidence that in recent years the leisure of retirement (to the extent that retirement brings leisure rather than a new set of obligations) is viewed both by retired people and by society at large as an earned privilege and opportunity (Atchley, 1971; Thompson, 1973). The "embarrassment" that has been cited as an obstacle to leisure participation among retired people is probably more a function of the poverty retirement often brings as opposed to being a function of embarrassment due to feelings of worthlessness brought on by leaving the job.[5]

Another source of embarrassment concerns the social context in which leisure skills must be learned by older adults. If leisure skills can be learned in an environment structured around the needs and abilities of older people, then embarrassment can be minimized. However, all too often older adults must learn in an environment developed to teach children—and that's embarrassing. Of course, another point is that taking the first few inept steps toward learning a new skill is *always* embarrassing, regardless of the age of the person trying to learn or his social position.

Situational Consequences

Admittedly, much of the preceding discussion reflects individual response to changes in situation. Nevertheless, there are three important situational changes related to retirement which deserve special attention: income changes, changes in residence, and changing family structure.

Income sources and strategies were dealt with in detail in an earlier chapter. In the present context my concern is with the social impact of the income changes which accompany retirement.

Obviously, retirement generally diminishes economic security. Income in retirement is usually about half what it was prior to retirement. Not only is income reduced, but feelings of economic deprivation increase (Riley and Foner, 1968: 455). However, feelings of economic deprivation tend to decrease in importance as the number of years of retirement increases.

Clark and Anderson (1967) found that reduced income had a significant impact on self-image, especially for people at the bottom of the socioeconomic scale. However, they conclude that life-long poverty has more impact on self-esteem than does a deteriorating standard of living.

Goldstein's (1960) work on consumption patterns of the aged gives us indirectly some useful evidence on the effect of income on spending choices. Comparing the consumption patterns of households with $5,000 annual income with those having only $1,000 annual income, Goldstein found that the major categories of expenditure for the two groups were similar: food and housing. While the low income households spent 38.9 percent of their incomes on food, the middle income households spent 32.3 percent on food. However, in absolute terms, the middle income households spent over *four times* as much per year on food compared to those with low incomes. Obviously, since nutrition is related to health and health is related to being able to play the role of retired person, the low income households suffer in terms of available nutritional energy. A person cannot burn up calories in activity if the calories are not there to burn, and prolonged calorie deficits produce the emaciated appearance of many of the older poor.

The low income households spent just over 70 percent of their incomes on food and housing, with just under $300 dollars per year left to be distributed among eight other categories of expenses. To get an idea of what this means, the middle income households spent fifteen times more money on travel and recreation each year than did the low income households. This was the point of widest differential in spending. It seems reasonable to conclude that people who are forced to live on very low incomes in retirement cut travel and recreation more than they do other categories. Thus, at a time in life when leisure opportunities are expanding, the resources necessary to take advantage of these opportunities decline for many retired people. For this reason, it is absolutely essential for us to know more about the role income plays in the management of choices in retirement.

Using a sample of 426 Senior Center participants, Peterson (1970) studied the perceptions of retired people concerning the adequacy of their incomes. He found that a majority of his sample viewed their current incomes as totally inadequate, and this was particularly true of blacks (84 percent), the unmarried (66 percent), women (60 percent), those with lower incomes (88 percent), those with less education (83 percent), and those who were completely retired (57 percent). Peterson's respondents also viewed the future with pessimism, especially those who saw their current incomes as inadequate. But only about a fifth felt that the adequacy of their incomes would actually *decline* in the future.

Change of residence is a change of circumstances which is closely associated with retirement in the minds of not only laymen, but professionals as well. For example, Arnold Rose (1965) saw the movement of older people to retirement communities as a major impetus for the development of an old age subculture. And because of their very high densities of older people, retirement communities such as Sun City, Arizona, and St. Petersburg, Florida, have perhaps commanded more attention than they deserve, given the fact that only a tiny proportion of the older population moves to such communities.

The fact of the matter is that while older people do move, only about 10 percent ever moves across county lines, and only about 2 percent ever moves across state lines. In addition, movers are not randomly distributed throughout the older population, but instead are concentrated among those who are widowed, disabled, retired, well-educated or living in households other than their own. When the effects of retirement alone are examined, it becomes clear that retirement has little impact on migration. The percentage that moves is slightly higher among retired people age sixty-five or over, as compared to those who are still on the job at that age, but the difference is significant only for men who move across county lines. There is very little impact of retirement on the movement of women or of men who move within the same county (Riley and Foner, 1968:149).

Educational attainment is a particularly important factor related to migration among older people. Long (1973) found that the probability that an older person will experience an inter-state move *in the rest of his life* is nearly four times higher for those who have some graduate education as compared to those who did not complete grammar school. However, for local moves, those with little education are much more likely to experience changes in residence. Long's data show that well-educated people are much more likely to experience long moves, while people with little education can expect a series of local moves, and people with high school or some college education can expect little movement after they reach age thirty-five.

Among those who do move, the reasons are not simple. Contrary to popular belief, Langford (1962) found that climate is one of the *least* important criteria influencing moves. The most important reason for moving is to secure a dwelling that is more suitable (clean, warm, smaller, etc.) for the household's current needs. Finding cheaper housing or lower taxes is the next most important reason for moving, followed by a desire to get away from deteriorating neighborhoods and a desire to move closer to family or friends. Thus, for those who do move, the characteristics of the particular housing unit and its relationship to community and family ties appear to be the salient factors involved in changes in housing. Other characteristics such as community facilities, climate, and topography are clearly less important.

It is also instructive to examine the reasons people gave for not wanting to move (Langford, 1962). People most often answered: "Because I don't want to, that's all." Langford classified this response as reflecting general satisfaction with the present situation. The specific answer most often given for not wanting to move was social ties with children, family, and friends (22 percent), followed by the characteristics of the neighborhood. These forces are apparently quite powerful, for only about a quarter of those who say they would be willing to move ever do (Riley and Foner, 1968: 153).

The most important point is that of the various factors which produce changes in residence in later life, retirement is of minor consequence. Only about 5 percent of those who do move across state lines move into retirement communities in what have come to be known as "retirement states" such as Florida, Arizona, or California. Likewise, the working-class retired who lead a gypsy-like existence, following the sun in travel trailers, are also an interesting but numerically insignificant portion of the retired population. The overwhelming majority of those who retire stay put. Those who do move do so for reasons other than a search for "retirement living." The most influential impact of retirement is to provide economic incentive to find less expensive housing, but this is usually found within the same general vicinity as preretirement housing.

The common notion that retirement brings on massive migrations is a myth. However, in the future, as the older population becomes more well-educated, the tendency to move at retirement may increase somewhat, but it is unlikely that this will ever become a prevalent trend.

Changing family structure is seldom brought on by retirement, but widowhood and the "empty nest" are two age-related factors which can coincide with retirement.

If most people are assumed to retire sometime between ages sixty-five and seventy, it is possible to examine the prevalence of various types of family situations which confront the retiring individual. In the age interval in which retirement most often occurs, 80 percent of the men are married, 10 percent widowed, and 10 percent single or divorced, and 52 percent of the women are married, 38 percent widowed and 10 percent single or divorced. Thus, the percentage of women who face retirement as widows is nearly four times higher than for men. What this means needs to be investigated. It may be that by removing the family supports, widowhood increases the probability of a difficult adjustment to retirement. On the other hand, having had to adjust to widowhood may have already prepared the individual for retirement. Probably the timing of widowhood and retirement in relation to one another is an important factor determining the impact of their interaction. Almost certainly the fact that a large proportion of women are widows when they retire is related to Streib and Schneider's (1971) finding of greater job deprivation among women.

If it occurs after retirement, widowhood can upset the adjustment an individual has made to retirement, and in some cases may force the individual to begin from scratch in developing a set of satisfying life activities. Just how this process works, we do not know either.

Ordinarily we do not think of the "empty nest," completion of the movement of grown children out of their parents' household, as a factor influencing retirement because the empty nest is a phenomenon which occurs for most parents long before retirement. However, to the extent that the job is used as a vehicle for adjusting to the empty nest, retirement can bring not only the problem of adjusting to retirement, but it may demand a new adjustment to the empty nest. The same would be true, of course, if the job had been used to compensate for widowhood.

Most retired people are married and living with a spouse. Retirement could be expected to affect the relationships within couples. Kerckhoff (1966) found that retiring husbands look forward to retirement, experience satisfaction in retirement, and are involved in the retirement process more as compared to their wives.[6] Compared to other couples with higher-level occupational background, those couples in which the husband was retiring or had retired from a semiskilled, unskilled, or service job were more passive in their anticipation of retirement. They also regarded retirement as an unpleasant experience, and they tended to view retirement much more negatively than did others.

Kerchkoff attributes this difference to the impact on the couple of the husband's greater involvement in household tasks following retirement. Among all occupational levels, retired men took a great part in household tasks after retirement. The difference was in how this increased household involvement was viewed. In the middle and upper strata, the increase was welcomed by the wives and seen as desirable by both husbands and wives. But the picture was different in the lower stratum; working-class marriages are less companionate and more authoritarian. Working class wives expect more exclusive control over the household. Indeed, before retirement, working-class men are much less involved in household affairs than are men in higher strata. Thus, upon retirement in the working class, both husbands and wives tend to see the husband's increased household involvement as undesirable. But the husbands increase their involvement despite themselves, which leads to conflict based on the guilt of the husbands and the irritation of the wives at having had their exclusive domain invaded.

Heyman and Jeffers (1968) also studied the impact of retirement on couples. They found that more than half of the wives were sorry that their husbands had retired. They also found that those who were sorry tended to be concentrated among the working class, those whose husbands were in poor health, and those who had had unhappy marriages before retirement.

It appears that retirement is a welcome change for couples in good health who enjoy middle or upper socioeconomic status. For those in poor health or those with working-class roots, however, retirement can have a negative effect on the couple.

In summary, retirement sometimes brings certain changes in situation which mean that the individual must not only adjust to retirement, but he must do it in an unfamiliar setting because of economic, household, or family factors.

Consequences for Society

As a social institution, retirement has some important consequences for society, including effects on communities, redistribution of population, and reduction of unemployment. The impact of retirement on communities has received little attention. There are a number of aspects to be examined.

Retirement creates a group of people for whom place of residence need have no relationship to the location of employment opportunities. For example, without retirement, many urban neighborhoods would have been completely deserted by the working class as the jobs moved steadily further outward from the central city. Another less important aspect of this issue is the fact that retired people are free to locate or to remain in areas off the beaten track, even within large urban areas.

Caliente is a good example of how the relocation process can work to society's advantage. In the late 1940's, Cottrell (1951) observed the impact on a small desert town in Nevada when the railroads changed from steam to diesel locomotives. When Caliente was eliminated as a service point on the transcontinental railway, the economic base of the town was destroyed. People who owned homes lost them, population moved out, the town seemed destined for oblivion. However, in 1969 Cottrell returned to Caliente and found the town flourishing (Cottrell, 1972). One facet in the rebirth of Caliente was a small but noticeable movement of retired people into the town. After the railroad left, the cost of housing hit bottom, and many retired people moved into the available homes. This had three results. It took advantage of existing housing which otherwise probably would have remained empty for some time, it brought a new source of income to Caliente, and it provided cheap housing for retired people.

While no concrete evidence is available on the extent to which this sort of process is occurring on a national scale, there can be little doubt that the existence of retirement incomes free from jobs has contributed to the ability of the central Midwest to hold its older population. And again this eases somewhat the pressure of people on low income housing in our larger urban areas.

The importance of retirement incomes to local areas is another topic which needs research attention. In our study of older people in Ohio (Atchley, et al., 1972) we found that $1,500,000,000 in income came into Ohio in 1970 from Social Security and Aid for the Aged *alone*. Seven Ohio counties had over $50,000,000 income each from these sources. Given the current ratio of Social Security to other retirement income, the total retirement income coming into Ohio in 1970 was about 3 billion dollars, a considerable amount of money. And this income was being spent within the state. Retired people are usually looked upon as representing an income problem, which they often do, but they also represent an important income source to a community, a fact which is less widely recognized.

Retired people also represent a more or less untapped manpower resource in local communities. As the results of the Foster Grandparent Program, Project Green Thumb, the Retired Senior Volunteer Program, and a host of other programs have shown, older citizens represent a highly capable pool of manpower. Ironically, the big difficulty at present in most communities is attitudes toward the use of retired citizens as manpower. Retired people frequently suffer as much frustration in trying to find satisfying and responsible volunteer positions as they do in trying to find paying jobs. In this instance, blind prejudice robs local communities of needed talent.

Finally, retirement is useful in industrial societies because it keeps the number of persons seeking jobs in reasonable balance with the number of available jobs. It also provides for an orderly way to avoid extensive retraining of older workers. These two functions are important in understanding the future of retirement. Because retirement is a means of adjusting the number of job seekers to the number of jobs, fluctuations in the number of jobs in relation to people can be expected to be accompanied by changing rules for retirement. In times of labor shortage, the rules for retirement may be tightened. In times of labor surplus, the rules for retirement may be liberalized. It is foolhardy to assume that retirement will continue automatically to exclude ever larger numbers of people from the labor force. Instead, it will continue to serve changing labor market needs in a changing industrial society. As the general level of education of the population improves, the problem of retraining older workers will become less difficult, and this may also, by removing some of the pressure for retirement, produce more flexible retirement procedures than we have now.

Students of social gerontology would do well to pay attention to the politics of retirement, for in the next two decades as the average age of the retired population increases, retirement is likely to become an even more lively political issue than it is now. For the most part, the courts and legislatures have both steadfastly avoided the question of the morality of compulsory retirement. Although recently the United States Supreme Court ruled that compulsory retirement was not unconstitutional, the issue still has several grounds yet to be argued before the high court. Yet as the retirement age creeps lower and compulsory retirement becomes more widespread, the probability that the issue will be forced into the open seems to be increasing.

Summary
Retirement has many particular personal consequences for the retirer. In examining these, it was found that retirement

generally has no adverse effect on physical health and if anything tends to improve it. Several studies have found that mental illness is more prevalent among the retired, but it is not clear just how much of this is due to retirement as opposed to other factors such as poor physical health, low social activity, or unsatisfactory living arrangement. To the extent that retirement removes the demands for rigid role conformity in public situations, it may well improve the level of functioning for those who are already mentally impaired.

Retirement has little effect on one's capacity for social adjustment. Morale, life satisfaction, self esteem, and hopefulness all show little change with retirement. Among men, however, retirement does increase the probability that age identification will be with the categories, old and very old. Most retired people show little job deprivation and a high degree of acceptance of retirement, and this proportion increases the longer a given retirement cohort has been retired.[7] Retirement produces little change in the percentage of Americans who report feelings of uselessness, but there is a slight tendency toward feelings of less involvement among men following retirement.

Retirement tends to produce no change in social participation. Where there is a change in social participation, it is generally an increase; in only a small minority of cases does retirement contribute to loneliness or social isolation. In retirement, social participation outside the family is to a great extent a function of occupation and particular national culture rather than a purely individual matter. A key determinant of social participation in retirement is having had an orderly work career which allows the development of ties with the community. Retirement results in an increased participation in leisure pursuits, and increasingly this move toward leisure is being defined by both retired people and the general public as a positive one.

Retirement also has other consequences. To the extent that it produces poverty, retirement restricts many of the individual's activities, particularly because of reduced food energy available, and drastically reduced allotments for recreation and travel. Retirement itself seldom produces changes in the community of residence. However, it may precipitate a search for more suitable housing within that community. Only about 2 percent of those who retire will ever move across state lines.

But, as the general educational level of the retired population increases, this percentage can be expected to increase. Somewhere around 40 percent of the women who retire are widows. For most couples, the "empty nest" is a familiar situation by the time of retirement. To the extent that increased involvement with the job is used as a mechanism for adjusting to widowhood or the empty nest, retirement may produce a delayed crisis of adjustment to those facts as well as to retirement itself. Retirement has a positive impact on couples in general, but among working-class couples, retirement often produces conflict.

Retirement also has consequences for society. By freeing people from the necessity to live close to their jobs, retirement increases the utilization of existing housing in central cities and in out-of-the-way places. Pensions also bring large amounts of disposable income into communities. Retirement is useful to society as a mechanism for keeping jobs and manpower in balance. Retired people represent a major untapped source of personnel for community service projects, but prejudice against the retired has only just begun to break down.

On balance, it would appear that the negative effects of retirement have been widely exaggerated. In addition, those problems that do come with retirement are not so much due to the inability of individuals to cope psychologically or physically with retirement but instead are due to a retirement institution which fails to deliver on the promised income security in retirement and to a system of age discrimination which denies retired people the opportunity to contribute to their communities in genuinely worthwhile ways. In short, the flaws are in the system, not in the people, and social and political policy (including law) are major factors which perpetuate the social inequities brought about by retirement.

9 • Adjustment to Retirement

The preceding chapter dealt with the detailed consequences of retirement. Now it is time to examine how people adjust to retirement itself. This is a field in which there has been a great deal of theorizing as well as systematic research. We will begin by examining the research findings on adjustment to retirement and then precede to an examination of various theories of retirement adjustment.

In our sample of retired teachers and telephone company employees (Cottrell and Atchley, 1969: 20), we found that nearly 30 percent felt they would never get used to retirement, and this percentage was higher among retired teachers. Streib and Schneider (1971) classified about 70 percent of their sample as being not completely satisfied with retirement.

Some people avoid the problems of adjusting to retirement by going back to a paying job. Streib and Schneider (1971: 145-158), in their longitudinal study of retirement, observed a number of people (about 10 percent) who returned to jobs after having retired. In examining the reasons for this return, they identified factors which *dispose* people to return to a job and factors which *allow* them to return. Those who are disposed to return are characterized by having had a negative attitude toward retirement, by attaching a positive value to the satisfactions of work, by having been forced to retire, and by having a high degree of felt economic deprivation. Also returnees tended to identify with the middle class and to have higher levels of education as compared to those who remained retired. In my research, I have found that those who hold jobs after retirement score very high on the job deprivation scale. Thus, the prime factors which dispose people to reject retirement appear to be a negative attitude toward it coupled with a tendency to feel deprived when not on the job. Low retirement income also provides incentive to reject retirement and seek a job.

Streib and Schneider found that the main factors which *allow* people to return to a job are good health and an upper-status occupation. My data also support these findings.

On the other hand, in our sample 49 percent reported that they got used to retirement in three months or less. Among retired men this percentage was 55, and among women, 45—a significant difference. Surprisingly, in our sample women consistently showed more difficulty adjusting to retirement than did men. Streib and Schneider found the same thing. Quick adjustment to retirement was related to having an adequate income and having had a semiskilled job.

Among those who encounter difficulty in adjusting to retirement, financial problems head the list (40 percent) followed by health problems (28 percent), missing one's job (22 percent), and death of spouse (10 percent) (Riley and Foner, 1968:453). Thus, of the 30 percent of retired people who have significant adjustment problems, only about 7 percent have problems of adjustment due to missing their jobs, while about 23 percent have adjustment problems which stem from the conditions under which the retirement role must be played.

Heidbreder (1972) examined white-collar/blue-collar differences in adjustment to early retirement. While she found that an overwhelming majority of people were satisfied with retirement, she also found that adjustment problems were concentrated among former blue-collar workers who had low incomes, poor health, and little education.

From the foregoing, it appears that not quite a third of the population has difficulty adjusting to retirement while over two-thirds do not. Hence, the crucial issues for the sociology of retirement are: why some people have difficulty adjusting to retirement and others do not; just what the individual must adjust to; and what processes are used by individuals to adjust to retirement.

At this point, there is insufficient information to allow construction of definitive theories of adjustment to retirement. Nevertheless, this does not remove the need for theory as a means of organizing research. In the paragraphs that follow, I will present what I consider to be some of the more promising ideas concerning adaptation to retirement. However, the reader should not lose sight of the fact that these ideas represent aids for organizing research, not a well-developed set of empirically derived and tested propositions.

Who Has Difficulty Adjusting?

It is probably safe to say that retirement causes a certain amount of disruption in the lives of just about everyone who retires. But why is this disruption so much more serious for some than for others? The answer to this is to be found by examining the relationship between the amount of change introduced by retirement and the capacity of the individual to deal with change routinely.

When people can deal with a substantial amount of change in a more or less routine fashion, we call them flexible. We also tend to think of changes as serious only if they exceed the level at which a person can deal with them routinely. People who have difficulty adjusting to retirement are often people with a low level of tolerance for any change. Obviously, the degree to which any change is serious depends on how adaptable the individual is. Thus, among those who have difficulty adjusting to retirement, we would expect to find a group of rigid, inflexible people for whom even small changes in the status quo are seen as serious. We would also expect to find a group of reasonably flexible people who are having to adjust to what seems to them a high magnitude of change.

Adjustment to What?

Retired people have only two things to adjust to that are directly related to retirement: loss of job and loss of income. In addition, retired people often find themselves having to adjust to declining health and to the loss of their spouses. However, these latter adjustments are related to retirement adjustment only in that they may occur at the same time and thus combine to produce a magnitude of change far greater than one of them is capable of producing alone.

The Process of Adjustment

As mentioned earlier, we have very little data on the processes whereby people adjust to a reduction in income. Almost certainly a decision-making model would be useful. What is needed is research to isolate the elements of choice in this particular framework. Very little is known about how decision-making priorities are set among people trying to adjust to reduced income.

More attention has been given to the problem of adjusting to the loss of one's job. Several theories of adjustment have emerged, each of which has a different emphasis.

Activity theory assumes that the job means different things to different people and that to adjust successfully to the loss of one's job, one must find a substitute for whatever personal goal the job was used to achieve. The most often quoted proponents of this theory are Friedmann and Havighurst (1954) and Miller (1965). Friedmann and Havighurst approach the matter in terms of substitute activities, and Miller carries it one step further to include substitute activities which serve as new sources of identity. The assumption here is that the individual will seek and find a work substitute. In a test of this theory, however, Shanas (1972) found it to be of very limited utility when applied to American society. In my own research, activity theory has fit the behavior of only a tiny proportion of retired people.

Continuity theory assumes that, whenever possible, the individual will cope with retirement by increasing the time spent in roles he already plays rather than by finding new roles to play (Atchley, 1972:35-36). This assumption is based on the finding that older people tend to stick with tried and true ways rather than to experiment, and on the assumption that most retired people want their life in retirement to be as much like their preretirement life as possible. However, the continuity theory allows for a gradual reduction in overall activity. Obviously, these basic assumptions do not fit *all* retired people, although they may fit the majority.

Disengagement theory (Cumming and Henry, 1961; Cumming, 1964; Henry, 1964) holds that retirement is a necessary manifestation of the mutual withdrawal of society and the older individual from one another as a consequence of the increased prospect of biological failure in the individual organism. This theory has been criticized for making the rejection of older people by society seem "natural" and, therefore, right. However, the fact of the matter is that many people do want to withdraw from full-time jobs and welcome the opportunity to do so. Streib and Schneider (1972) refined disengagement theory to apply more directly to the realities of retirement. *Differential disengagement* is the term they use to reflect the idea that disengagement can occur at different rates for different roles. And they do not contend that disengagement is irreversible. They hold that by removing the necessity for energy-sapping labor on a job, retirement may free the individual with declining energy to increase his level of engagement in other spheres of life. Earlier we found that such increases in involvement do in fact occur.

Thus, both continuity theory and the theory of differential disengagement attempt to explain why people do not adjust to retirement as activity theory or disengagement theory would lead us to expect.

A Theory of Adjustment

Hazardous as it may be, I would like to offer yet another theory of adjustment to retirement. It is to some extent speculative, but I think it is also based on the facts as we now know them. It also synthesizes the major elements of the three theories mentioned above. In this theory the central processes of adjustment are *internal compromise* and *interpersonal negotiations*. While these two elements of the theory interact quite strongly in real situations, for analytical purposes, I shall treat them separately. When a person retires, a new role is taken on and an old one relinquished, at least to some degree. The extent to which this triggers a need for the person to adjust depends on how the job role fits into his pattern of adjustment prior to retirement. Everyone has personal goals—goals which, if achieved, give the individual a strong sense of personal worth or satisfaction. These goals are of several types. Some of them involve learning to respond to life in a particular manner by developing certain personal qualities, such as honesty, ambition, cheerfulness, kindness, and so on. Other personal goals are materialistic and involve achieving ownership of particular property such as land, house, stereo, car, etc. Still other personal goals involve successfully playing certain roles. Thus, a person's desire to succeed as a parent, a job-holder, an artist, or in any number of other roles may be viewed also in relation to this hierarchy of personal goals.

These various types of goals differ a great deal in terms of their transferability and their capacities as enduring sources of satisfaction. Materialistic goals seem to be the most transitory, because after they are achieved, they often turn to ashes in the mouth of the achiever. This process of disillusionment can take some time, however, and many people have materialistic goals they never achieve. Thus, while this type of goal may be the least substantial, it seems to be a common goal in American society. And to the extent that lowered income in retirement interferes with materialistic goals not yet achieved, retirement can trigger adjustment problems.

Personal goals that are related to success in various roles are less concrete than materialistic goals. The object of materialistic goals is obvious, but the criteria for successful role playing can be illusory indeed. While this means that the individual often cannot be sure whether he has or has not been a success as a role player it also means that he is much more free to decide for himself. Also, the fruits of successful role playing can be savored long after the success is achieved. In fact, often such successes literally improve with distance from achievement as the negative aspects are forgotten and only the positive ones remain in one's memories.

Goals related to personal qualities are often more difficult to achieve, but at the same time are less vulnerable to changing circumstances. It may be difficult to *become* a cheeful person, but if one *is* a cheerful person, this characteristic tends to carry over to all kinds of situations. Thus, if one is, and wants to be, intelligent, friendly, kind, neat, honest and self-assured, these achievements are valued in any situation. On the other hand, it is difficult, although not impossible, to learn to be self-confident if one is not already disposed in that direction.

An individual's personal goals are organized into a hierarchy which indicates his priorities for achieving them. This hierarchy reflects the relative importance of particular personal goals. The hierarchy and the personal goals that compose it constantly change as goals are added or dropped and as success or failure alters priorities. Personal goals come from three major sources: goals we are taught and are expected to hold as personal goals; personal goals which are held by others we seek to emulate; and personal goals which grow out of our own experiences and knowledge about ourselves and our capabilities. Any or all three sources in various combinations may contribute to motivation toward a given personal goal.

The hierarchy of personal goals is influenced by a number of factors. Sex and age norms are particularly pertinent. Males may run into trouble if they attempt to take on full-time child rearing as a top priority personal goal. Likewise, females may run into trouble if they want to be auto mechanics. Norms also exist concerning the hierarchy most appropriate at various ages. As a child, the individual finds that such goals as learning manners, developing various personal qualities such as trustworthiness, and gaining basic skills for adulthood are the main types of personal goals which society holds out to him as important. There is normally a complete absence of concern with matters such as marriage, parenthood, or career at the top of the child's working, day-to-day goal structure. On the other hand, a twenty-eight-year-old man preoccupied with learning to play hop-scotch would be considered weird indeed, for we would expect him to have mastered the skills involved much earlier. Thus, an important aspect of many personal goals is that once they are achieved they can be given a lower priority, although they may remain important. The norms demand that upon retirement, the job is no longer eligible to occupy a top spot in the hierarchy of personal goals, and factors such as managing one's own affairs and maintaining an independent household are moved up on the list of expected priorities. And this is becoming increasingly true.

But the norms about the hierarchy of personal goals often tell the individual more about what he cannot do than about what he can do, and usually the individual still has plenty of choices, even, within the bounds of what is allowable for a given sex at a given stage in the life cycle. Much of the task of matching the individual's capabilities and interests to the options that are available as personal goals is left up to the individual. Family, school, friends, bosses, and co-workers exert influence along the line to be sure, but in the final analysis, the individual must make his own internal compromises if he is to become a self-sufficient adult. Of course, some people never make it this far and remain creatures of the demands placed on them in the situation of the moment.

For our purposes, the most important compromises involve the top priority *roles* in the hierarchy. The individual starts off

in adolescence with a tentative hierarchy. To the extent that he
can gain experience through school, summer jobs or other means
concerning how workable the tentative hierarchy of roles is,
the individual can gradually move toward stabilizing the hierarchy, particularly the top-priority roles. This sort of stability
is important at this stage because it gives the budding adult
the security of a firm sense of purpose, of knowing where he is
going.

Such stability in the hierarchy of personal goals may be
achieved in two ways. The hierarchy may be positively rein-
forced, become satisfying, meet with success, and therefore,
attract the individual's commitment. Or the hierarchy may
produce results that are neither bad enough tocause it to be
abandoned nor good enough to merit the individual's commitment, but at the same time the hierarchy may have been used
long enough to have become a habit. For prople who are committed to a hierarchy with the job at or near the top, retirement
is more difficult than for people for whom the job is a prime
consideration only out of habit. Of course, retirement is but
one of many changes that *can* destory the stability of one's
hierarchy of personal goals. Whether retirement *does* destory
this stability depends on where the job role fits into this hierarchy.

For people who stress personal qualities, the job may be
quite far down on the list. Materialistic people may consider
the job more important, to the extent that it governs ability to
achieve materialistic goals. Even among people who judge their
successes primarily in terms of role performance, however, the
job may not be a primary source of satisfaction.

Figure 3 shows a schematic diagram of how retirement effects
the hierarchy of personal goals. It shows the points at which
internal compromise becomes necessary as a mechanism of
adjustment to retirement. Retirement obviously introduces a
change. The crucial question, however, is whether retirement
is a *consequential* change, a change that is important enough to
necessitate a reorganization in the upper level of the individual's
hierarchy of personal goals. If not, then retirement produces no
actual change in the criteria the individual uses to select from
among the behavioral alternatives available to him. People who
strive mainly to develop personal qualities are particularly
likely to find themselves in the latter situation. People for whom
roles other than the job are more important could also fit into

Figure 3. Effect of Retirement on Personal Goals

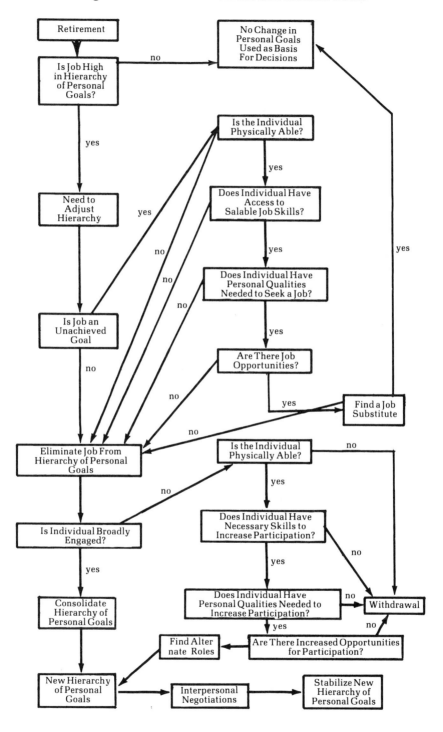

this particular category. The same may be true for people who have given the job a top priority but who also have achieved their ambitions regarding the job.

For many people, however, retirement does involve some amount of reorganization in their hierarchy of personal goals. If the job is very high on the list of personal goals, and yet unachieved, the individual can be expected to try to replace it with a substitute job. Ability to accomplish this is directly related to the degree to which the necessary personal and circumstantial prerequisites are present. First, the individual must be physically able to take up a new job. He must also have or be able to get job skills that are salable in the job market. He must also have other personal qualities such as the self-confidence and drive which are necessary in seeking a new job.[1] But most important, there must be job opportunities. If all of these conditions can be satisfied, then the individual can find a substitute job which allows him to retain his hierarchy of personal goals intact. Of course, this may be a temporary response since retirement becomes a necessity for virtually everyone who lives long enough.

If any one of the prerequisities for finding a substitute job cannot be satisfied, then the individual will be unable to find one and must reorganize his hierarchy of personal goals. If the job is not very high in the hierarchy, but high enough to cause a need for reorganization, then the individual proceeds directly with reorganizing his hierarchy of personal goals and does not try to find a substitute job.

If the individual is broadly engaged (Cumming, 1964) in a number of roles other than the job role, then the reorganization will simply take the form of consolidating the remaining roles within the hierarchy of personal goals. Suppose a person's hierarchy of personal goals looked like this, with the most important at the top:

Being a decent, honest person
Being a good husband
Having a comfortable, well-furnished home
Being a good golfer
Being a good neighbor
Being a successful insurance salesman
Keeping a lid on his temper

Improving himself through reading
Being a dutiful son-in-law to his wife's mother

Obviously, retirement need make little change in the essential hierarchy. None of the top items would be disturbed by retirement although reduced income might interfere with his standards for his house and his golf. In this case, there is really no need to search about for new alternatives. There are many there already. This is essentially the model used in continuity theory.

If, on the other hand, the individual is narrowly engaged (Cumming, 1964), his hierarchy of personal goals might look like this:

Being a successful corporation president
|
|
|
|
|
|
Being a good husband

The dotted line is there to indicate distance and also to indicate that a large number of personal goals, both qualitative and materialistic, are tied to success on the job. For this type of individual, retirement eliminates not only the job but several other goals as well. And it leaves very little. In this situation, the individual was involved in the job at the exclusion of everything else, and as a result must find alternatives to replace the job in his hierarchy of personal goals. The extent to which this task can be accomplished depends again on the individual's having the necessary physical energy, skills, personal qualities and opportunities. Failure to satisfy any of these prerequisites will necessarily result in withdrawal. This is the model of disengagement theory. Success gives the individual the materials with which to forge a new hierarchy of personal goals. This is the model of activity theory. The theory of differential disengagement leads us also to expect that the individual will often undergo a net decline in activity even if the hierarchy of goals is successfully reorganized.

The process involved in developing or changing the hierarchy of personal goals is, of course, decision-making, and the expression *internal compromise* is used to describe this decision-making process in order to indicate that its outcome is far from determinate. The process by which people reorganize their criteria for decision-making is one we know too little about.

An important aspect of all this is just where the retired role (as opposed to the job role) fits into this hierarchy. Some people may resist including successful retirement in their hierarchy of personal goals at all. Still others may put it at the bottom. Increasingly, however, playing the role of retired person seems to be taking a high position in the hierarchy and, therefore, can be expected to play a part in the reorganization of the hierarchy. Research is needed to establish just where the retirement role fits into the structure of personal goals and under what circumstances its rank may vary.

Interpersonal negotiation is a process in which the individual discusses his goals and aspirations with those of the people he interacts with. It is through this process that the world outside the individual can influence development of and change in his hierarchy of personal goals. When we say that we "know" a person, one of the things we "know" is his hierarchy of personal goals. When this hierarchy changes, the individual indicates to others, through the decisions he makes or through his actions, that a change has taken place. I use the term negotiation here because often the individual runs into resistance in getting others who are important to him to accept his new hierarchy of personal goals. And at this point, the results of internal compromise and feedback from significant others enter into a dialectic.

Unfortunately, while I can assert with a high degree of confidence that this interpersonal negotiation process is important to the developing of a stable hierarchy of personal goals in retirement, the research evidence is too meager to provide many clues as to how this process works and how retirement and job roles are dealt with in the process. This problem illustrates the importance of basic descriptive research to the theory-building enterprise, for while sufficient facts were present to allow a fairly explicit theory of internal compromise to be developed, no such facts were available with respect to interpersonal negotiations. Theory and research must be developed hand-in hand. And endeavors which become overbalanced in either direction tend to be less useful than a balanced progression.

Summary
(Not quite a third of the retired population encounters difficulty in adjusting to retirement.) Adjusting to reduced income is by far the most frequently encountered difficulty (40 percent). Missing one's job accounts for about 22 percent of the adjustment difficulties. The remaining 38 percent is accounted for by factors such as death of spouse or declining health which are directly related to retirement adjustment only in that they influence the situation in which retirement adjustment must be carried out. This suggests that certain situational prerequisites are often necessary for a good adjustment.

From a positive point of view, it seems safe to say that adjustment to retirement is greatly enhanced by sufficient income, the ability to gracefully give up one's job, and good health. In addition, adjustment seems to be smoothest when situational changes other than loss of job are at a minimum. Another way of viewing this is to say, assuming that one's fantasy concerning the retirement role is based on reality, that factors which upset the ability of the retirer to live out his retirement ambitions hinder his ability to adjust retirement smoothly.

People who have difficulty adjusting to retirement tend to be those who are either very inflexible in the face of change, or faced with substantial change, or both. The prime things about retirement that must be adjusted to are loss of income and loss of job. We know very little about how people adjust to loss of income.

Adjustment to loss of job through retirement has been the subject of a fair amount of research and theory. Activity theory assumes that the job will be replaced with some other role and that activity level will stay about the same. Continuity theory assumes that overall activity level may go down and that increased participation will take place among roles already played rather than among new roles. Disengagement theory assumes that the job role will simply be dropped without any appreciable change in activity in other roles and without any attempt to replace the job role.

An original theory of adjustment was presented which attempts to synthesize various theories by relating them to changes in the individual's hierarchy of personal goals. This theory of internal compromise and interpersonal negotiations is both complex and comprehensive, yet it is also specific enough to be testable. It is suggested as a possible focus for further research on adjustment to retirement.

10 • The Future of Retirement

In the foregoing chapters I have tried to organize our knowledge about retirement in such a way that the reader could become aware of just what we did and did not know. More than once I have speculated about various aspects of retirement chiefly in the hope that some of these speculations might trigger research efforts, but also because I enjoy speculation.

In this chapter, I am going to speculate about the future of retirement. My educated guesses are probably as educated as anyone's could be at this point, but they are still guesses.

Manpower and Public Policy

At the societal level, retirement is primarily a mechanism for adjusting the supply of labor to the demand. Retirement policy has this goal as its basis, although it is seldom so explicitly stated. Therefore, a crucial issue in the future of retirement in American society is what is going to happen to the supply of and demand for people to hold jobs.

In my opinion, the pressure to keep older people out of the labor force which has been so very strong for the past thirty years may lessen. The basis for this opinion is two assumptions: that energy shortages will slow down the development of automation and that the decline in the birth rate will eventually reduce the supply of people entering the labor market. These two factors will, I believe, combine to produce incentive for keeping older workers in the labor force.

It is quite true that there are other groups such as women, members of minority groups, and the hard-core unemployed which will vie for any increase in available jobs. And in the past, these groups have been able to push out older workers because jobs were changing fast and older workers were not prepared education-wise for a world in which the nature of jobs was constantly changing. In the future, however, older workers can be expected to be better educated and more accustomed to the flexibility required by changing jobs. As a result, retaining older workers may be much more attractive to employers in the future than it is today.

The pressures to retain older workers probably will not be the same in all areas of the economy. Jobs can be divided into two groups: capital intensive and labor intensive. In capital intensive jobs, almost all of the energy used to do the job comes from nonhuman sources. These are jobs where machines and electricity, bought with capital, do the producing, and human beings serve mainly as guides, coordinators or attendants. In those jobs which have been or can be automated, there will continue to be little need for the labor of older adults. In labor-intensive jobs, on the other hand, people provide most of the energy to get the job done. These are the kind of jobs held by professionals, skilled craftsmen, tradesmen, service workers, many clerical workers, etc. The service sector of the American economy is growing faster than any other at present, and it is in this sector particularly that the older worker can expect pressure *against* retirement to increase.

Retirement policy can therefore be expected to become more flexible than it is today. Because retirement as an earned right has become institutionalized in American society, it will probably be politically impossible to eliminate it entirely. Nor would this be desirable. What *can* change is the typical age at which retirement is allowed, or the age at which it is demanded. It is quite possible that both of these ages could increase.

Another policy change which may take place in the face of a need for continued labor by older workers is a change in the all-or-nothing nature of retirement policy. Currently workers generally work full-time, year-round or not at all. In the future, policy may well become more flexible to allow people to work half-days or a limited number of days a week. Such a change would very likely be successful in retaining older workers because it would allow them the flexibility to adjust to their need to increase the time they spend on things other than work, or their need to compensate for declines in health or available energy. At the same time, it would meet their desire to maintain at least some involvement with the job.

A key policy which affects retirement is the level of Social Security pensions. Unlike an insurance policy which is a contract in which the insured knows the day he signs the contract what he can expect to receive, Social Security is a public pension system which is constantly being changed through legislation. So far, this feature has been a boon to retired people. But in the future, if "the public good" demands it, the rules for collecting pensions under Social Security could be changed to reduce the incentive for retirement that Social Security pensions represent. For example, elimination of early retirement provisions would accomplish such a purpose. It would be unwise for any student of retirement to lose sight of the fact that Social Security pension levels are not acts of God but are instead mere creatures of the political process.

Economic Support for Retired People

Income represents the foremost problem retired people have at present, and in the future this problem is apt to become even more widespread. Inflation is a serious threat particularly to those who must live on pensions and annuities which cannot change as prices change. Social Security pensions have a built-in mechanism for cost-of-living increases.

Equally important is what is going to happen to the need for income as the average age of the retired population increases. At a certain point, aging forces the individual to abandon going up on the roof to fix a leak, mowing the grass, or getting on a ladder to take down drapes for spring housecleaning. Thus, as age increases, a whole host of services must be bought that were formerly done by household members themselves. This increase in the cost of living is partially offset by reductions in money spent for other items such as travel, but not completely by any means.

Likewise, as the retired population increases in average age, the number requiring expensive medical care and long-term institutionalization will also increase. Of course, at this point the individual will probably have left the retirement role and taken up a sick or disabled role; but he will still rely primarily on his retirement pension for income. The issue here is that income levels necessary to support people in independent retirement are insufficient to meet the needs of people who live beyond retirement more dependent roles.

The strategy which will be used to increase the level of income support for retired people will probably not involve an increase in employee or employer contributions alone. Recently, a new philosophy for Social Security has emerged which involves using general tax revenues to supplement Social Security pensions. Some people who will qualify for payments under this new scheme will not be entitled to benefits based on prior work experience but on the basis of age alone. This will have the advantage of wiping out some of the inequities in earnings that existed during the years when most people have employment, but it will also move Social Security pensions away from being entirely retirement pensions. Just how this may affect public acceptance of the legitimacy of Social Security is unclear. For the select few, the maturity of private pension programs will widen the gap between single-pension and dual-pension households even further.

Regardless of the ins and outs of retirement income strategy, pension levels will probably not increase very much in terms of purchasing power. There simply does not appear to be the political power necessary to bring about such an increase. On the other hand, should the purchasing power of pensions fall much below their current levels, organized political pressure for better pensions could emerge. Perversely, it would seem that in the long run it might be easier to increase pension levels if they were reduced somewhat now. Certainly, average pension levels will not exceed the bare minimum in the foreseeable future at the rate things have been going. The political implications of this trend will be interesting to follow, and perhaps horrifying too.

Retirement and the Individual

In the future, we can look for an increase in the effectiveness of all types of retirement preparation. However, the informal socialization that grows out of observing retired people in action is likely to be particularly important. At this writing, I am at a stage in life in which my parents and the parents of most people my age are retired or nearing retirement. As I talk to people about my work, I am impressed with the extent to which direct experience with retired people allows people to identify both the prerequisites for playing the retirement role and the obstacles people encounter in the process. These experiences are widespread and they both sensitize people to their own eventual retirement and motivate them to construct realistic fantasies about retirement.

The future will also bring an increase in formal retirement preparation programs, and these programs will be better in the future as more is learned about retirement. A notable change will be the trend toward emphasizing the positive features of retirement rather than the negative. Formal programs also can be expected to incorporate more concrete ideas about how to meet the prerequisites for playing the retirement role.

Acceptance of retirement will increase in the future. By the year 2000, everyone reaching retirement age in the United States will have been born into a social world in which retirement and Social Security are taken for granted. Also, as experience in dealing with retirement builds, more concrete standards for playing the retirement role may emerge. While this may cut down on the flexibility retirement currently allows, it will also reduce the number who see retirement as moving into a vague unknown. However, the level of acceptance of retirement will be most directly influenced by the level of pension incomes. As long as pensions stay at least as adequate as they are today, then acceptance of retirement will increase, as will the desire for earlier retirement.

In my opinion, the changes in the Social Security funding base will have little impact on the acceptance of retirement. Most Americans look upon Social Security as legitimate and it is to their advantage to continue to do so.

As acceptance of retirement by the general public increases and as we begin to know more about its positive side, the retirement event can be expected to become a more balanced, more prospective event than it has been in the past. In general, however, retirement ceremonies will probably still be rather uncomfortable events, unless they are personalized experiences involving a small group of friends.

In the future, retirement will be less and less a traumatic aspect of life. At present, only about 30 percent of retiring persons have serious problems associated with retirement, and the percentage will decrease in the future so long as pensions remain at their present level or higher. As the average level of education among retired people increases, there will be more changes in residence following retirement, particularly across state lines. There will also be a trend toward more active utilization of retired people as a manpower resource for community projects. The decline of the negative stereotype associated with retirement should reduce the present unwillingness to put retired people into responsible volunteer posts.

As time goes by, there should be a reduction in the differentials in the outcome of retirement which occur as a consequence of sex or social class. Growing equality between the sexes should reduce the differential impact of retirement on men and women. Increased acceptance of retirement should reduce job deprivation among those who retire from upper-level professional and technical jobs. The general rise in educational level should provide working-class retirers with better leisure skills. These two trends will substantially reduce the two most prevalent negative consequences of retirement.

In the future, the retirement role will be increasingly expected to occupy one of the top spots in the hierarchy of personal goals of the retired person. Over time, the proportion of the retired population narrowly engaged primarily in job roles can be expected to decline in prevalence, at least to the extent that problems arise from missing one's job. Income represents the factor with the most potential to increase problems of retirement adjustment. Once again pension levels are vital. In the future poor health and loss of spouse can both be expected on the average to occur later in life. This means that they will be less likely to interfere with retirement adjustment unless the typical retirement age also increases.

The foregoing comments are certainly speculative, and they represent only what I consider to be some of the more important changes which may occur in the future of retirement. Yet I felt an urge to include them by way of tying together the points made earlier in the separate chapters. In the next section of this final chapter, I would like to turn to the question of needs related to retirement. Research needs, program needs, and training needs will each be considered. The idea in presenting this last section is to illustrate that knowledge carries with it the obligation of considering where to go from here.

Research Needs

This book identifies a very large number of more or less specific areas in which additional research is needed. I will not try to recapitulate all of them here in the full context in which they were identified. I will instead present them as a sort of "shopping list" to refresh the reader's memory.

These are a few areas in need of further research:

What have been the consequences of the lack of agreement on an operational definition of retirement?

What is the most effective way to sample the retired population?

What is the relationship between economic development and the institutionalization of retirement?

What cross-national similarities or differences exist with respect to retirement and why?

What is the relationship between political development and the institutionalization of retirement?

What is the nature of the linkage between people and their jobs and how does this linkage change?

How do men and women differ in terms of attitude toward or adjustment to work and retirement?

What are the mechanisms through which people are informally socialized for retirement and how effective are they?

Why do most people refuse to participate in retirement preparation programs if they are available?

How do people manage to counteract the negative stereotype of retirement and come out with a positive attitude toward it?

To what extent do negative stereotypes influence the outcome of retirement?

How do attitudes of family and/or friends influence a worker's decsion to retire?

What effects do occupational norms concerning the desirability of retirement affect an individual retiring from that occupation in terms of attitude toward or adjustment to retirement?

What impact does the presence or absence of leisure skills have on willingness to retire?

Why does increased age produce increased willingness to retire?

What impact does job discrimination have on acceptance of or adjustment to retirement?

To what extent is a flexible retirement system feasible at the societal level?

What determines the content and meaning of a retirement ceremony?

What differences exist in the probability that retiring workers will experience a retirement ceremony?

What is the last day on the job typically like and what impact does this have on attitudes toward or adjustment to retirement?

What determines what the last day on the job will be like?

What roles do gifts play in the retirement process?

How is the retirement role defined and what impact does this have on the retirement process?

What systematic differences exist in how the retirement role is defined and why?

What are the dynamics of self and role in later life, and how do they influence the retirement process?

What role does fantasy play in the retirement process?

What phases exist in the retirement process and why?

How do people adjust to reduced incomes in retirement?

What impact will the aging of the retired population have on pension adequacy?

What is the feasibility of various strategies for increasing retirement income levels?

To what extent do people adopt the sick role rather than the retirement role and why?

What is the relationship between retirement and mental disorders?

What systematic differences exist in terms of the impact of retirement on social participation or social isolation?

What role does income play in the management of choices in retirement?

To what extent is retirement affected by widowhood or vice versa?

To what extent do pensions provide economic resources for isolated communities?

What are the economic costs and/or benefits of having retired people in the community?

Why are communities reluctant to use retired people in responsible volunteer positions in public projects?

To what extent is retirement sensitive to fluctuations in the age-sex distribution of the population?

To what extent are "minority problems" present in the retirement institution and why?

What factors determine the salience of retirement as a political issue and why?

How adequate is Atchley's theory of adjustment to retirement?

This is just a partial list. Many of the statements are generalized to include several possible research problems. These questions alone could generate over two hundred separate research studies just to get the topics covered, not to mention covering various sub-populations. In addition, most of the research that has been done on retirement so far needs to be repeated several times in order to be conclusive. The upshot is that the field of retirement research is about as open as it could possibly be.

Program Needs

The 1971 White House Conference on Aging identified a large array of program needs of the older population, which, of course, includes most retired people. However, here we will be concerned only with identifying a few program needs directly related to retirement.

Many people need assistance in coping with reduced incomes in retirement. Programs to assist people in financial management and in consumer protection are particularly worth trying. Counselling and referral services are also useful in this respect. Local Social Security offices often perform such services.

Recreational programs such as those found in Senior Centers serve the needs of those who need help in filling the time gap left by leaving their jobs. More of these centers are cropping up all the time, and in the future, the all-purpose Senior Center may become recognized as a logical meeting place for retired people with similar interests. Thus far, however, Senior Centers and old age clubs have met with only limited success in reaching the general retired population. Perhaps better outreach services would improve the track record of Senior Centers.[1]

Most agencies and programs which are directed toward older people are only indirectly concerned with problems of retirement. That there is little demand on social agencies for such services probably reflects a view on the part of retired people that solving retirement problems is an individual responsibility.

The major program need, therefore, lies in the area of retirement preparation programs. There is an especially great need for community-sponsored programs to serve those who cannot get such programs at their places of employment. There is also a need for introducing people to some of the realities of retirement in the public elementary and secondary schools. Much of the information contained in this book should be common knowledge by the time a person becomes an adult.

Training Needs

There are not many training needs directly related to retirement. Certainly there is a need for more researchers studying retirement. Researchers with sufficient background in sophisticated social science methodology are particularly lacking. But there are few training needs of researchers that are unique to the study of retirement.

There is a need for better training for professionals and practitioners concerning retirement. Psychiatrists and physicians in particular seem to have a jaundiced view of retirement. Also, public school teachers, professors, social workers, lawyers, and many others need to be oriented toward the facts rather than the myths concerning retirement.

However, there is a particularly strong need for training those who will offer retirement planning programs. Demand for such programs is escalating, yet there is little in the way of organized training for those who will end up being responsible for them. Those training programs that do exist sometimes emphasize the less practical goal of counseling and neglect the more realistic goals of providing information and stimulating the person to plan his own retirement. And most tend to still be overly concerned with the negative aspects of retirement to the exclusion of its positive aspects.

A Personal Epilogue

Writing this book has been fun but at times nervewracking. As a friend of mine once said, "It is a somewhat unnerving sensation to undertake a study which one knows will be attacked, whatever the results." On the one hand, there is enough information about retirement available to fill several books, but on the other hand, it would take a hundred books to fill all the gaps in our knowledge about retirement.

I see this book as serving three purposes: summarizing the existing research literature, providing a framework through which retirement can be seen as a complex and evolving social phenomenon, and identifying conspicuous gaps in our knowledge about retirement. To the extent that these objectives have been achieved, I will consider my job to be done.

BIBLIOGRAPHY

Acuff, Gene, and Donald Allen.
    1970. "Hiatus in 'Meaning': Disengagement for Retired Professors." *Journal of Gerontology*, 25:126-128.

Atchley, Robert C.
    1974. "The Meaning of Retirement." *Journal of Communication*, 24:4:97-100.

————. and Linda K. George
    1973. "Symptomatic Measurement of Age." *Gerontologist*, 13:332-336.

————.
    1972a. *The Social Forces in Later Life: An Introduction to Gerontology.* Belmont, California: Wadsworth.

———— , Fred Cottrell, Linda K. George, and Ruth W. Smith
    1972b. *Ohio's Older People.* Oxford, Ohio: Scripps Foundation for Research in Population Problems.

————.
    1971a. "Disengagement among Professors." *Journal of Gerontology*, 26:476-480.

————.
    1971b. "Retirement and Leisure Participation: Continuity or Crisis?" *Gerontologist*, 11:(1, part I), 13-17.

————.
    1971c. "Retirement and Work Orientation." *Gerontologist*, 11:(1, part I), 29-32

————.
    1969. "Respondents vs. Refusers in an Interview Study of Retired Women." *Journal of Gerontology*, 24:42-47.

135

———.
   1967.   *Retired Women: A Study of Self and Role.* Unpub-
            lished Ph. D. dissertation. Ann Arbor, Michigan:
            University Microfilms.
Back, Kurt W.
   1969.   "The Ambiguity of Retirement." In E. W. Busse and
            Eric Pfeiffer (eds.), *Behavior and Adaptation in Late
            Life*, pp. 93-114.
———, and Carleton S. Guptill.
   1966.   "Retirement and Self-Ratings." In Ida H. Simpson and
            John C. McKinney (eds.), *Social Aspects of Aging.*
            Durham, North Carolina: Duke University Press,
            pp. 120-129.
Ball, Robert M.
   1973.   Testimony before the United States Senate Special
            Committee on Aging. In *Future Directions in Social
            Security.* Washington, D. C.: United States Senate
            Special Committee on Aging, pp. 13-61.
Barfield, Richard E.
   1969a. *The Automobile Worker and Retirement.* Ann Arbor,
            Michigan: University of Michigan, Institute of Social
            Research.
———, and James Morgan.
   1969b. *Early Retirement: The Decision and the Experience.*
            Ann Arbor, Michigan: Institute of Social Research.
Barron, Milton L., Gordon F. Streib, and E. A. Suchman.
   1952.   "Research on the Social Disorganization of Retirement."
            American Sociological Review, 17:479-482.
Bauder, Ward W., and Jon A. Doerflinger.
   1967.   "Work Roles among the Rural Aged." In E. Grant
            Youmans (ed.), *Older Rural Americans*, Lexington,
            Kentucky: University of Kentucky Press, pp. 22-43.
Belbin, R. Meredith, and F. LeGros Clark.
   1970.   "The Relationship between Retirement Patterns and
            Work as Revealed by the British Census." *Industrial
            Gerontology,* 4:12-26.
Bellino, Robert.
   1970.   "Perspectives of Military and Civilian Retirement."
            Mental Hygiene, 54:580-583.
Bengtson, Vern L.
   1969.   "Differences between Subsamples in Level of Pres-

ent Role Activity." In Robert J. Havighurst, *et al.*
(eds.), *Adjustment to Retirement: A Cross-National
Study*, New York: Humanities Press, pp. 35-49.

Biderman, Albert D., and Laurie M. Sharp.
1968. "The Convergence of Military and Civilian Occupational Structures—Evidence from Studies of Military
Retirement Employment." *American Journal of Sociology*, 73:381-399.

Bixby, Lenore E.
1972. "Women and Social Security in the United States."
Social Security Bulletin, 35:September, 3-11.

_____, and Virginia Reno.
1971. "Second Pensions among Newly Entitled Workers:
Survey of New Beneficiaries." *Social Security Bulletin*,
34:November, 3-7.

_____.
1970. "Income of People Aged 65 and Older: Overview from
the 1968 Survey of the Aged." *Social Security Bulletin*,
April, 1970:3-34.

_____, and Lola M. Irelan.
1969a. "The Social Security Administration Program of
Retirement Research." *Gerontologist*, 9:143-147.

_____, and E. Eleanor Rings.
1969b. "Work Experience of Men Claiming Retirement Benefits, 1966." *Social Security Bulletin*, 32:August, 3-14.

Blau, Zena S.
1956. "Changes in Status and Age Identification." *American Sociological Review*, 21:198-203.

Brotz, Edward L.
1968. "Retirement and the Individual." *Journal of the
American Geriatrics Society*, 16:1-15.

Breen, Leonard Z.
1963. "Retirement—Norms, Behaviour, and Functional
Aspects of Normative Behavior." In Richard H.
Williams, *et al.* (eds.), *Processes of Aging, Volume II*,
New York: Atherton Press, pp. 381-388.

Bretz, Judith S.
1969. "Beneficiaries with Minimum Benefits: Work History
of Retired Workers Newly Entitled in 1966." *Social
Security Bulletin*, 32: December, 36-47.

Brodsky, Carroll M.
   1971. "Compensation Illness as a Retirement Channel."
         Journal of the American Geriatrics Society, 19:51-60.
Bultena, Gordon L.
   1969a. "Health Patterns of Aged Migrant Retirees." *Journal
         of the American Geriatrics Society*, 17:1127-1131.
   _____, and Vivian Wood.
   1969b. "Normative Attitudes toward the Aged Role among
         Migrant and Nonmigrant Retirees." *Gerontologist*,
         9:(3, part I), 204-208.
Burgess, Ernest W.
   1960. *Aging in Western Societies*. Chicago: University of
         Chicago Press.
Carp, Frances M.
   1972. *Retirement*. New York: Behavioral Publications.
   _____.

   1968. *The Retirement Process*. Washington, D. C. : United
         States Government Printing Office.
Charles, Don C.
   1971. "Effect of Participation in a Pre-retirement Program."
         Gerontologist, 11:(1, part I), 24-28.
Chen, R.
   1968. "The Emotional Problems of Retirement." *Journal
         of the American Geriatrics Society*, 16:290-295.
Chen, Yung-Ping.
   1966. "Low Income, Early Retirement, and Tax Policy."
         Gerontologist, 6:35-38.
Clague, Ewan.
   1971. "The Private Pension Dilemma." *Industrial Geron-
         tology*, 11:1-9.
Clare, James L.
   1971. "Age 65—Too Young to Retire?" *Pension and Welfare
         News*, 7:12:40, 42, 70, 74.
Clark, Margaret, and Barbara Anderson.
   1967. *Culture and Aging*. Springfield, Illinois: Charles C.
         Thomas.
Cloninger, Dale O.
   1971. "Employer Attitudes and Practices in Employment
         of the Retired." Abstract. *Industrial Gerontology*, 8:40.
Cohen, Wilbur J.
   1970. "Social Security—The First Thirty-five Years." In:

Occasional Papers in Gerontology No. 7. Ann Arbor, Michigan: University of Michigan—Wayne State University Institute of Gerontology, pp. 1-32.

Cottrell, Fred.
1972. *Technology, Man, and Progress.* Columbus, Ohio: Charles E. Merrill.

———, and Robert C. Atchley.
1969. *Women in Retirement: A Preliminary Report.* Oxford, Ohio: Scripps Foundation for Research in Population Problems.

———.
1955. *Energy and Society.* New York: McGraw-Hill.

———.
1951. "Death by Dieselization: A Case Study in the Reaction to Technological Change." *American Sociological Review,* 16:358-365.

Cowgill, Donald O., and Lowell D. Holmes.
1972. *Aging and Modernization.* New York: Appleton-Century-Crofts.

Crawford, Marion P.
1972. "Retirement and Role-Playing." Abstract. *Industrial Gerontology,* 15:90-91.

Cumming, Elaine.
1964. "New Thoughts on the Theory of Disengagement." In Robert Kastenbaum (ed.), *New Thoughts on Old Age,* New York: Springer.

———, and William E. Henry.
1961. *Growing Old: The Process of Disengagement.* New York: Basic Books.

Davidson, Wayne R.
1969. "Some Observations about Early Retirement in Industry." *Industrial Gerontology,* 1:26-30.

———, and Karl R. Kunze.
1965. "Psychological, Social, and Economic Meanings of Work in Modern Society: Their Effects on the Worker Facing Retirement." *Gerontologist,* 5:129-133.

Distefano, M. K.
1969. "Changes in Work Related Attitudes with Age." *Journal of Genetic Psychology,* 114:127-134.

Donahue, Wilma T., Harold Orbach, and Otto Pollak.
1960. "Retirement: The Emerging Social Pattern." In Clark

Tibbitts (ed.), *Handbook of Social Gerontology,* Chicago: University of Chicago Press, pp. 330-406.

Draper, J. E., E. F. Lundgren, and G. B. Strother.
1967.   *Work Attitudes and Retirement Adjustment.* Madison, Wisconsin: University of Wisconsin Bureau of Business Research and Services.

Eisdorfer, Carl.
1972.   "Adaptation to Loss of Work." In Frances M. Carp (ed.), *Retirement,* New York: Behavioral Publications, pp. 245-266.

Ellison, David L.
1968.   "Work, Retirement and the Sick Role." *Gerontologist,* 8:189-192.

Epstein, Lenore, and Janet H. Murray
1968.   "Employment and Retirement." In Bernice L. Neugarten (ed.), *Middle Age and Aging,* Chicago: University of Chicago Press, pp. 354-356.

————.
1966.   "Early Retirement and Work-Life Experience." *Social Security Bulletin,* 29:March, 3-10.

Fields, Theron J.
1970.   "Company-Initiated Early Retirement as a Means of Work-Force Control." Abstract. *Industrial Gerontology,* 4:36-38.

Fillenbaum, Gerda G.
1971a. "A Consideration of Some Factors Related to Work after Retirement." *Gerontologist,* 11:18-23.

————.
1971b. "On the Relation between Attitude to Work and Attitude to Retirement." *Journal of Gerontology,* 24:244-248.

————.
1971c. "Retirement Planning Programs—At What Age, and for Whom?" *Gerontologist,* 11:33-36.

————.
1971d. "The Working Retired." *Journal of Gerontology,* 26: 82-89.

Friedmann, Eugene, and Robert J. Havighurst. (eds.)
1954.   *The Meaning of Work and Retirement.* Chicago: University of Chicago Press.

Gallaway, Lowell E.
    1965. "The Retirement Decision: An Exploratory Essay."
        *Social Security Administration Research Report
        No. 9.* Washington D. C.: United States Government
        Printing Office.
Goldstein, Sidney
    1960. *Consumption Patterns of the Aged.* Philadelphia:
        University of Pennsylvania Press.
Gordon, Margaret S.
    1963. "Income Security Programs and the Propensity to
        Retire." In Richard H. Williams, Clark Tibbitts, and
        Wilma Donahue (eds.), *Processes of Aging,* Vol. II.,
        New York: Atherton Press, pp. 436-458.
    _____.
    1961. "Work and Patterns of Retirement." In Robert W.
        Kleemeier (ed.), *Aging and Leisure,* New York: Ox-
        ford University Press, pp. 15-53.
Green, Mark R., *et al.*
    1969. *Pre-retirement Counseling, Retirement Adjustment
        and the Older Employee.* Eugene, Oregon: University
        of Oregon Graduate School of Management.
Hanson, Pamela Marsters.
    1972. "Age and Physical Capacity to Work." *Industrial
        Gerontology,* 12:20-28.
Havighurst, Robert J., *et al.* (eds.)
    1969. *Adjustment to Retirement: A Cross-National Study.*
        New York; Humanities Press.
    _____, Bernice L. Neugarten, and Vern L. Bengston.
    1966. "A Cross-National Study of Adjustment to Retire-
        ment." *Gerontologist,* 6:137-138.
Heidbreder, Elizabeth M.
    1972a. "Factors in Retirement Adjustment: White-Collar/
        Blue-Collar Experience." *Industrial Gerontology,*
        12:69-79.
    _____.
    1972b. "Pensions and the Single Woman." *Industrial Geron-
        tology,* 15:52-62.
Henry, William E.
    1971. "The Role of Work in Structuring the Life Cycle."
        Human Development, 14:125-131.

———.
  1965. "The Theory of Intrinsic Disengagement." In P. From
         Hansen (ed.), Age with a Future, Copenhagen: Munks-
         gaard. pp. 415-418.
Heron, Alastair.
  1963. "Retirement Attitudes among Industrial Workers
         in the Sixth Decade of Life." Vita Humana, 6:152-159.
Heyman, Dorothy K., and Frances C. Jeffers.
  1968. "Wives and Retirement: A Pilot Study." Journal of
         Gerontology, 23:488-496.
Hunter, Woodrow W.
  1968. A Longitudinal Study of Pre-Retirement Education.
         Ann Arbor, Michigan: University of Michigan Di-
         vision of Gerontology.
Hurwitz, Jacob C., and Willie L. Burris.
  1972. "Terminated UAW Pension Plans: A Study." Industrial
         Gerontology, 15:40-51.
Industrial Gerontology, The Editors.
  1973. "Approaching Retirement Age: Attitudes toward
         Older Workers and Retirement Policies in Three
         Companies." Industrial Gerontology, 16:1-13.
Irelan, Lola M., and Dena K. Motley.
  1972. "Health on the Threshold of Retirement." Industrial
         Gerontology, 12:16-19.
Jacobson, D.
  1972. "Willingness to Retire in Relation to Job Strain and
         Type of Work." Industrial Gerontology, 13:65-74.
Jaffe, A. J.
  1971. "Has the Retreat from the Labor Force Halted? A
         Note on Retirement of Men, 1930-1970." Industrial
         Gerontology, 9:1-12.

———.
  1970. "Men Prefer not to Retire." Industrial Gerontology,
         5:1-11.

———.
  1968. "Differential Patterns of Retirement by Social Class
         and Personal Characteristics," In Frances M. Carp
         (ed.), The Retirement Process, Washington, D. C.:
         United States Government Printing Office, pp. 105-110.
Kaplan, T. S.
  1971. "Too Old to Work: The Constitutionality of Manda-

tory Retirement Plans." *Southern California Law Review,* 44:150-180.

Kasschau, Patricia L.
1974. Reevaluating the Need for Retirement Preparation Programs." *Industrial Gerontology,* New Series, 1:1:42-59.

Katona, George, James N. Morgan, and Richard E. Barfield.
1969. "Retirement in Prospect and Retrospect." In *Occasional Papers in Gerontology No. 4,* Ann Arbor, Michigan: University of Michigan - Wayne State University Institute of Gerontology, pp. 27-49.

Kerckhoff, Alan C.
1966. "Family Patterns and Morale in Retirement." In Ida H. Simpson and John C. McKinney (eds.), *Social Aspects of Aging,* Durham, North Carolina: Duke University Press, pp. 173-194.

————.
1964. "Husband-Wife Expectations and Reactions to Retirement." *Journal of Gerontology,* 19:510-516.

King, Charles E. and William H. Howell.
1965. "Role Characteristics of Flexible and Inflexible Retired Persons." *Sociology and Social Research,* 49:153-165.

Kleemeier, Robert W.
1964. "Leisure and Disengagement in Retirement." *Gerontologist,* 4:180-184.

Kohn, Melvin L., and Carmi Schooler.
1973. "Occupational Experience and Psychological Functioning: An Assessment of Reciprocal Effects." *American Sociological Review,* 38:97-118.

Kolodrubetz, Walter W.
1970. "Private and Public Retirement Pensions: Findings from the 1968 Survey of the Aged." *Social Security Bulletin,* 33: September, 3-22.

Koyl, Leon F.
1970. "A Technique for Measuring Functional Criteria in Placement and Retirement Practices." In Harold L. Sheppard (ed.), *Industrial Gerontology.* Cambridge, Massachusetts: Shenkman, pp. 140-156.

Kreps, Juanita M.
1968a. "Comparative Studies of Work and Retirement."

In Ethel Shanas and John Madge (eds.), *Problems in Cross-National Studies in Aging*, New York: S. Karger, pp. 75-99.

———.

1968b. *Lifetime Allocation of Work and Leisure.* Social Security Administration Research Report No. 22. Washington, D. C.: Government Printing Office.

———.

1966. "Employment Policy and Income Maintenance for the Aged." In John C. McKinney and Frank DeVyver (eds.), *Aging and Social Policy*, New York: Appleton-Century-Crofts, pp. 136-157.

———(ed.).

1964. *Technology, Manpower, and Retirement Policy.* Cleveland, Ohio: World Publishing Co.

———.

1963. *Employment, Income, and Retirement Problems of the Aged.* Durham, North Carolina: Duke University Press.

Lambert, Edouard.

1964. "Reflections on a Policy for Retirement." *International Labour Review*, 90:365-375.

Langford, Marilyn.

1962. *Community Aspects of Housing for the Aged.* Research Report No. 5. Ithaca, New York: Cornell University Center for Housing and Environmental Studies.

Laroque, Pierre.

1972. "Women's Rights and Widow's Pensions." *International Labour Review*, 106:1-10.

Laurence, Mary W.

1961. "Sources of Satisfaction in the Lives of Working Women." *Journal of Gerontology*, 16:163-167.

Lauriat, Patience.

1970a. "Benefit Levels and Socio-Economic Characteristics: Findings from the 1968 Survey of the Aged." *Social Security Bulletin*, 33:August, 3-20.

———, and William Robin.

1970b. "Men Who Claim Benefits before Age 65: Findings from the Survey of New Beneficiaries, 1968." *Social Security Bulletin*, 33:November, 3-29.

Long, Larry H.
   1973. "Migration Differentials by Education and Occupation: Trends and Variations." *Demography*, 10:243-258.
Lowenthal, Marjorie F.
   1964. "Social Isolation and Mental Illness in Old Age." *American Sociological Review*, 29:54-70.
_____, and Paul L. Berkman.
   1967. *Aging and Mental Disorder in San Francisco*. San Francisco: Jossey-Bass.
McEwan, Peter J. M., and Alan P. Sheldon.
   1969. "Patterns of Retirement and Related Variables." *Journal of Geriatric Psychiatry*, 3:35-54.
McMahan, C. A., and T. R. Ford.
   1955. "Surviving the First Five Years of Retirement." *Journal of Gerontology*, 10:212-215.
Maddox, George L.
   1968. "Retirement as a Social Event in the United States." In Bernice L. Neugarten (ed.), *Middle Age and Aging*, Chicago: University of Chicago Press, pp. 357-365.
Martin, John, and Ann Doran.
   1966. "Evidence Concerning the Relationship between Health and Retirement." *Sociological Review*, 14:329-343.
Mathiasen, Geneva.
   1953. *Criteria for Retirement*. New York: G. P. Putnam's Sons.
Messer, Elizabeth F.
   1969. "Thirty Years Is a Plenty." In *Occasional Papers in Gerontology No. 4*, Ann Arbor, Michigan: University of Michigan - Wayne State University Institute of Gerontology, pp. 50-66.
Michelon, L. C.
   1954. "The New Leisure Class." *American Journal of Sociology*, 59:371-378.
Miller, Stephen J.
   1965. "The Social Dilemma of the Aging Leisure Participant," In Arnold M. Rose and Warren A. Peterson (eds.), *Older People and Their Social World*, Philadelphia: F. A. Davis, pp. 77-92.

Mills, C. Wright.
    1959. *The Sociological Imagination.* New York: Oxford
    University Press.

————.
    1956. *White Collar.* New York: Oxford University Press.
Mitchell, William L.
    1968. *Preparation for Retirement.* Washington, D. C. Amer-
    ican Association of Retired Persons.
Monk, Abraham.
    1972. "A Social Policy Framework for Pre-retirement
    Planning." *Industrial Gerontology,* 15:63-70.

————.
    1971. "Factors in the Preparation for Retirement by Middle-
    Aged Adults." Gerontologist, 11:(4, part I), 348-351.
Morse, Nancy C., and Robert S. Weiss.
    1955. "The Function and Meaning of Work and the Job."
    American Sociological Review, 20:191-198.
Motley, Dena K.
    1972. "Health in the Years before Retirement." *Social
    Security Bulletin,* 35:December, 18-36.
Murray, Janet.
    1972. "Homeownership and Financial Assets: Findings
    from the 1968 Survey of the Aged." *Social Security
    Bulletin,* 35:August, 3-23.
Myers, Robert J.
    1954. "Factors in Interpreting Mortality after Retirement."
    Journal of the American Statistical Association,
    49:499-509.
Nadelson, Theodore.
    1969. "A Survey of the Literature on the Adjustment of
    the Aged to Retirement." *Journal of Geriatric Psy-
    chiatry,* 3:3-20.
Orbach, Harold L.
    1969. "Social and Institutional Aspects of Industrial
    Workers' Retirement Patterns." In *Occasional Papers
    in Gerontology No. 4,* Ann Arbor, Michigan: Univer-
    sity of Michigan - Wayne State University Institute
    of Gerontology, pp. 1-26.

————.
    1967. "Social and Institutional Aspects of Industrial
    Workers' Retirement." In *Retirement and the Individ-*

ual, U. S. Senate Special Committee on Aging, Washington, D. C.: United States Government Printing Office, pp. 533-560.

———. 1963. "Social Values and the Institutionalization of Retirement." In Richard H. Williams, *et al.* (eds.), *Processes of Aging, Volume II*, New York: Atherton Press, pp. 389-402.

Organisation for Economic Cooperation and Development.
1970. *Flexibility of Retirement Age*. Paris: The Organisation.

Owen, John P., and L. D. Belzung.
1967. "Consequences of Voluntary Early Retirement: A Case Study of a New Labour Force Phenomenon." *British Journal of Industrial Relations*, 5:162-189.

Paillat, P.
1971. "The Cost of the Advancement of Retirement Age in Industrialized Countries." In *Work and Aging*, Paris: International Centre For Social Gerontology, pp. 39-53.

Palmore, Erdman.
1972. "Compulsory Versus Flexible Retirement: Issues and Facts." *Gerontologist*, 12:4:343-348.

———. 1971. "Why Do People Retire." *Aging and Human Development*, 2:269-283.

———. 1967. "Employment and Retirement." In Lenore Epstein (ed.), *The Aged Population of the United States*, Washington, D. C.: United States Government Printing Office.

———. 1965. "Differences in the Retirement Patterns of Men and Women." *Gerontologist*, 5:4-8.

———. 1964. "Retirement Patterns among Aged Men: Findings of the 1963 Survey of the Aged." *Social Security Bulletin*, 27:August, 3-10.

Peterson, David A.
1972. *The Crisis in Retirement Finance: The Views of Older Americans*. Ann Arbor, Michigan: University of Michigan - Wayne State University Institute of Gerontology.

Pfeiffer, Eric, and G. C. Davis.
   1971.   "The Use of Leisure Time in Middle Life." Gerontologist,
           11:187-195.
Pollak, Otto.
   1956.   The Social Aspects of Retirement. Homewood,
           Illinois: R. D. Irwin.
Pollman, A. William.
   1971a. "Early Retirement: A Comparison of Poor Health to
           Other Retirement Factors." Journal of Gerontology,
           26:41-45.

_____.
   1971b. "Early Retirement: Relationship to Variation in Life
           Satisfaction." Gerontologist, 11:(1, part I), 43-47.
Powers, Edward A., and Willis H. Goudy.
   1971.   "Examination of the Meaning of Work to Older Work-
           ers." Aging and Human Development, 2:38-45.
Pyron, H. Charles, and U. Vincent Manion.
   1970.   "The Company, the Individual, and the Decision to
           Retire." Industrial Gerontology, 4:1-11.
Reichard, Suzanne, Florine Livson, and Paul G. Petersen.
   1968.   "Adjustment to Retirement." In Bernice L. Neugarten
           (ed.), Middle Age and Aging, Chicago: University of
           Chicago Press, pp. 178-180.
Reno, Virginia P.
   1972.   "Compulsory Retirement among Newly Entitled
           Workers: Survey of New Beneficiaries." Social Secur-
           ity Bulletin, 35:March, 3-15.

_____.
   1971a. Retirement Patterns of Men at OASDHI Entitlement.
           Washington, D. C.: United States Government Print-
           ing Office.

_____.
   1971b. "Why Men Stop Working at or before Age 65." Social
           Security Bulletin, 34: April, 3-17.
_____, and Carol Zuckert.
   1971c. "Benefit Levels of Newly Retired Workers: Findings
           from the Survey of New Beneficiaries." Social Security
           Bulletin, 34:July, 3-31.
Riley, Matilda W., and Anne E. Foner.
   1968.   Aging and Society: Volume I, An Inventory of Re-
           search Findings. New York: Russell Sage Foundation.

Rollins, Boyd C., and Harold Feldman.
1970.   "Marital Satisfaction over the Family Life Cycle."
        Journal of Marriage and the Family, 32:20-28.
Rose, Arnold M.
1965.   "The Subculture of the Aging: A Framework for
        Research in Social Gerontology." In Arnold Rose and
        Warren A. Peterson (eds.), *Older People and Their
        Social World*, Philadelphia: F. A. Davis, pp. 3-16.
Rose, Charles L., and John M. Mogey.
1972.   "Aging and Preference for Later Retirement." *Aging
        and Human Development*, 3:45-62.
Rosenberg, George S.
1970.   *The Worker Grows Old*. San Francisco: Jossey-Bass.
Rosenberg, Morris.
1964.   *Society and the Adolescent Self-Image*. Princeton,
        New Jersey: Princeton University Press.
Rowe, A. R.
1972.   "The Retirement of Academic Scientists." *Journal
        of Gerontology*, 27:113-118.
Schneider, Clement J.
1964.   *Adjustment of Employed Women to Retirement*. Ph. D.
        dissertation, Cornell University (unpublished).
Schuchat, T.
1971.   "Postponed Retirement under the Social Security Act."
        Industrial Gerontology, 11:20-22.
Schulz, James H., and Guy Carrin.
1972.   "The Role of Savings and Pension Systems in Main-
        taining Living Standards in Retirement." *Journal of
        Human Resources*, 7:343-365.

———.

1970.   *Pension Aspects of the Economics of Aging: Present
        and Future Roles of Private Pensions*. Washington,
        D. C.: United States Senate Special Committee on
        Aging.
Seltzer, Mildred M., and Robert C. Atchley.
1971.   "The Impact of Structural Integration into the Pro-
        fession on Work Commitment, Potential for Disen-
        gagement, and Leisure Preferences among Social
        Workers." *Sociological Focus*, 5: Autumn, 9-17.
Shanas, Ethel.
1972.   "Adjustment to Retirement: Substitution or Accomo-

dation?" In Frances M. Carp (ed.), *Retirement.* New York: Behavioral Publications, pp. 219-244.

_____.

1971. "Disengagement and Work: Myth and Reality." In *Work and Aging,* Paris: International Centre of Social Gerontology, pp. 109-119.

_____, et al.

1968. *Old People in Three Industrial Societies.* New York: Atherton Press.

Sheppard, Harold L., and Michel Philibert.

1972. "Employment and Retirement: Roles and Activities." *Gerontologist,* Summer, part II, 29-35.

_____.

1971. *New Perspectives on Older Workers.* Washington, D. C.: W. E. Upjohn Institute for Employment Research.

Shultz, Edwin B.

1963. *A Study of Programs of Preparation for Retirement in Industry.* Ithaca, New York: Cornell University, New York State School of Industrial and Labor Relations.

Simpson, Ida H.

1969. "Problems of the Aging in Work and Retirement." In Rosamonde R. Boyd and G. C. Oakes (eds.), *Foundations of Practical Gerontology,* Columbia, South Carolina: University of South Carolina Press, pp. 151-166.

_____, Kurt W. Back, and John C. McKinney.

1966a. "Continuity of Work and Retirement Activities, and Self-Evaluation." In Ida H. Simpson and John C. McKinney (eds.), *Social Aspects of Aging,* Durham, North Carolina: Duke University Press, pp. 106-119.

_____, _____, and _____.

1966b. "Exposure to Information on, Preparation for, and Self-Evaluation in Retirement." In Ida H. Simpson and John C. McKinney (eds.), *Social Aspects of Aging,* Durham, North Carolina: Duke University Press, pp. 90-105.

_____, _____, and _____.

1966c. "Orientation toward Work and Retirement, and Self-Evaluation in Retirement." In Ida H. Simpson and John C. McKinney (eds.), *Social Aspects of Aging,*

Durham, North Carolina: Duke University Press, pp. 75-89.

———, ———, and ———.

1966d. "Work and Retirement." In Ida H. Simpson and John C. McKinney (eds), *Social Aspects of Aging*, Durham, North Carolina: Duke University Press, pp. 45-54.

———, and John C. McKinney (Eds.)

1966e. *Social Aspects of Aging*. Durham, North Carolina: Duke University Press.

Slavick, Fred.

1966. *Compulsory and Flexible Retirement in the American Economy*. Ithaca, New York: Cornell University Press.

———, and Seymour L. Wolfbein.

1960. "The Evolving Work-Life Pattern." In Clark Tibbitts (ed.), *Handbook of Social Gerontology*, Chicago: University of Chicago Press, pp. 298-329.

Smith, P. C., et al.

1969. *The Measurement of Satisfaction in Work and Retirement: A Strategy for the Study of Attitudes*. Chicago: Rand McNally.

Social Security Administration.

1970. *Annual Statistical Supplement*. Washington, D. C.: United States Government Printing Office.

Stanford, E. P.

1971. Retirement Anticipation in the Military." *Gerontologist*, 11:37-42.

Steiner, Peter O., and Robert Dorfman.

1957. *The Economic Status of the Aged*. Los Angeles: University of California Press.

Stokes, Randall G., and George L. Maddox.

1967. "Some Social Factors in Retirement Adaptation." *Journal of Gerontology*, 22:329-333.

Streib, Gordon F., and Clement J. Schneider.

1972. *Retirement in American Society*. Ithaca, New York: Cornell University Press.

———.

1965. "Intergenerational Relations: Perspective of the Two Generations." *Journal of Marriage and the Family*, 27:469-476.

———, Wayne E. Thompson, and E. A. Suchman.

1958a. "The Cornell Study of Occupational Retirement." *Journal of Social Issues*, 14:3-17.

———.

1958b. "Family Patterns in Retirement." *Journal of Social Issues,* 14:46-60.

———, and Wayne E. Thompson.

1957. "Personal and Social Adjustment in Retirement." In Wilma Donahue and Clark Tibbitts (eds.), *New Frontiers of Aging,* Ann Arbor, Michigan: University of Michigan Press, pp. 180-197.

———.

1956. "Morale of the Retired." *Social Problems,* 3:270-276.

Tatzman, Manfred.

1972. "How to Prevent Retirement Shock." Abstract. *Industrial Gerontology,* 16:89.

Taylor, Charles.

1972. "Developmental Conceptions and the Retirement Process." In Frances M. Carp (ed.), *Retirement,* New York: Behavioral Publications, pp. 75-116.

Thompson, Gayle B.

1973. "Work Versus Leisure Roles: An Investigation of Morale among Employed and Retired Men." *Journal of Gerontology,* 28:339-344.

Thompson, Wayne E., Gordon F. Streib, and John Kosa.

1960. "The Effect of Retirement on Personal Adjustment: A Panel Analysis." *Journal of Gerontology,* 15:165-169.

———.

1958a. "Pre-retirement Anticipation and Adjustment in Retirement." *Journal of Social Issues,* 14:35-45.

———, and Gordon F. Streib.

1958b. "Situational Determinants: Health and Economic Deprivation in Retirement." *Journal of Social Issues* 14:18-34.

Tibbitts, Clark.

1960. *Handbook of Social Gerontology.* Chicago: University of Chicago Press.

———.

1954. "Retirement Problems in American Society." *American Journal of Sociology,* 59:301-308.

Tissue, Thomas.

1970. "Downward Mobility in Old Age." *Social Problems,* 18:67-77.

Tuckman, Jacob, and Irving Lorge.
  1953. *Retirement and the Industrial Worker.* New York: Columbia University Teacher's College.
Tyhurst, James S., Lee Salk, and Miriam Kennedy.
  1957. "Mortality, Morbidity, and Retirement." *American Journal of Public Health,* 47:1434-1444.
United States Department of Labor, Labor Management Services Administration.
  1969. *The 100 Largest Retirement Plans: 1960-1968.* Washington, D. C.: United States Government Printing Office. United States Senate Special Committee on Aging.
  1967. U.S. Senate Special Committee on Aging. *Retirement and the Individual.* (Vols. 1 and 2). Washington, D.C.: United States Government Printing Office.
Vogel, Bruce S., and Robert E. Schell.
  1968. "Vocational Interest Patterns in Late Maturity and Retirement." *Journal of Gerontology,* 23:66-70.
Wentworth, Edna C.
  1968. *Employment after Retirement: A Study of Post-Entitlement Work Experience of Men Drawing Benefits under Social Security.* Washington, D. C.: United States Government Printing Office.
Williams, Richard H., and Claudine Wirths.
  1965. *Lives through the Years.* New York: Atherton Press.

NOTES

NOTES TO CHAPTER 1

1. Although some authors are beginning to use *life-course* in preference to *life cycle* on the grounds that life-course is more accurately descriptive, I have chosen to continue to use life cycle, as defined in biology, to refer to the entire series of processes constituting the life history of an organism.

2. For an excellent discussion of this issue see Phillips (1973).

3. *Empirical* means based on sensory experience. Thus, to "know" something empirically one must be able to see, feel, smell, hear, or taste it. This criterion means that most mystical or religious explanations cannot qualify as scientific.

4. Weeks not worked was 52 minus number of weeks of full-time work and minus one-half the number of weeks of half-time or part-time work.

5. I recognize that using he, him, and his for singular individuals, sex unspecified, is contributing to the perpetuation of sexism in the English language. I was tempted to use tem, tey, and teir as has been suggested by some, but the thought of all those footnotes caused me to abandon the idea.

6. Students of the social aspects of aging, which includes retirement.

NOTES TO CHAPTER 2

1. For an excellent discussion of the impact of this process, see Cottrell (1955).

2. While the preceding account may give the impression that these changes occurred smoothly, it should be borne in mind that we have centered on the outcomes of industrialization which led to the develop-

ment of retirement, and as a result, we have neglected the detailed processes and conflicts which led to these outcomes. For example, it took a civil war, a severe economic depression, and several decades of conflict to create a strong national government in the United States, and the rise of the labor unions was a long and often violent struggle. For understanding retirement, however, it is probably more useful to know what the outcomes were rather than the fine details of how they were achieved.

NOTES TO CHAPTER 3

1. This category includes clerks, salesmen, skilled workers and foremen.

2. Includes executives, professionals, and government officials.

3. Includes mainly factory operatives and some non-household service workers.

NOTES TO CHAPTER 4

1. There is a large amount of literature emerging on early retirement. (Barfield and Morgan, 1969; Fields, 1970; Davidson, 1969; Owen and Belzung, 1967; Biderman and Sharp, 1968; Reno, 1971; Pollman, 1971; Paillat, 1971; Messer, 1969; Katona, Morgan and Barfield, 1969; Orbach, 1969; Epstein, 1966; Chen, 1966; and Barfield, 1970). However, as yet we know very little about the impact of early retirement. When the experience with early retirement has accumulated to a much greater extent than it has up until now, will we be in a much better position to assess the pros and cons.

2. Streib and Schneider (1971) have suggested that *administrative* retirement may be a better word than *compulsory* or *mandatory* retirement since many people are relieved to reach the mandatory retirement age. However, whether the individual welcomes retirement or not, the mandatory age is a disqualifying rule.

3. This means that periods of severe chronic illness and disability tend to occur at a later age now than they did in the past. Thus, today's seventy-year-old is more vigorous and healty than a seventy-year-old in 1935.

4. *Age differences* are differences among people of various ages. Age differences, say the difference in 1970 in measured intelligence between people born in 1900 and people born in 1930, can be the result of aging or the fact that people born in different eras grow up in different economic, social, and educational systems (the cohort effect). This type of research is referred to as *cross-sectional* because it studies a cross-section of ages at a single point in time. *Age changes* are differences for

the *same individuals* at different ages, say the differences in measured intelligence in a group of people born in 1930 and measured at ages 20 and 40. This type of research is called *longitudinal* because it involves following a cohort of people (people born in the same year) through time. The problem with this approach is that it does not allow comparisons *between* cohorts. *Cross-sequential* research allows the researcher to control the cohort effect while examining age changes. Several cohorts are followed through time just as in longitudinal research, but the investigator compares age changes built up from the experience of several cohorts. For example, if we are interested in looking at age changes from age 50 to age 70 with cohort effects controlled, then we could build up a set of data on 50-year-olds and a set of data for 70-year-olds. The differences observed would be due to age changes and not the unique experience of any single cohort. Obviously, the greater the period over which cross-sequential age data can be collected, the more the cohort effect is minimized. None of these designs is fool-proof, but longitudinal or cross-sequential designs are vastly superior to cross-sectional designs for studying changes due to aging.

NOTES TO CHAPTER 5

1. This idea was suggested by Nan Corby.

NOTES TO CHAPTER 6

1. Jobs also have important qualitative aspects, but these are seldom emphasized in "job descriptions" or in discussion about jobs, and this is perhaps a major oversight.

2. The initial outline for this section developed out of discussions with my colleague at the Scripps Foundation, Mildred M. Seltzer.

3. The term *disenchantment* was suggested by Vi Sobers, a lively retired nurse, who professed to be in this phase at the time she took my course on retirement at the 1973 Summer Institute for Study in Gerontology at the University of Southern California.

4. The *role-set* is the group of people with whom one must interact in carrying out a particular role.

NOTES TO CHAPTER 7

1. These regulations are constantly changing. Contact the Social Security Administration for the latest regulations.

2. The median is the income figure which splits the frequency distribution of incomes into two equal halves, one above and one below the median.

3. These estimates are adjusted to reflect the 1967 value of the dollar.

NOTES TO CHAPTER 8

* Statements in parentheses are those which were coded as "positive answers" to the scale item.

1. Coding refers to the process whereby raw data is assigned numbers or combined or otherwise transformed into a form suitable for analysis.

2. This finding matches Thompson (1958) and Streib and Schneider (1971).

3. They demanded a scale score of zero for "low job deprivation" while Simpson, Back, and McKinney used 0-2, as I did.

4. Austria, West Germany, the Netherlands, Italy, Poland and the United States.

5. For a more thorough discussion of this issue see Atchley (1971b).

6. Kerckhoff did not ascertain whether the wives themselves were also engaged in retirement from jobs of their own.

7. A cohort is a group of people who share a given characteristic such as retirement during the same period of time.

NOTES TO CHAPTER 9

1. This factor was suggested by Helena Lopata.

NOTES TO CHAPTER 10

1. *Outreach services* identify people in need of a given program or service and actively go to them to solicit their participation.